The American Ambulance

1900 through 2002
An Illustrated History

Walter M.P. McCall

Iconografix

Iconografix
1830A Hanley Road
Hudson, Wisconsin 54016 USA

Library of Congress Card Number: 2002104773

ISBN 1-58388-081-X

Reprinted November 2012

Printed in The United States of America

Cover and book design by Shawn Glidden

Copyedited by Suzie Helberg

BIBLIOGRAPHY

The Professional Car, the Quarterly Magazine of The Professional Car Society, Inc.

American Funeral Cars & Ambulances Since 1900, by Thomas A. McPherson, Crestline Publishing, 1973.

Classic American Ambulances 1900-1979 Photo Archive, by Walt McCall and Tom McPherson, Iconografix, Inc., 1999.

Classic American Funeral Vehicles 1900-1980 Photo Archive, by Walt McCall and Tom McPherson, Iconografix, Inc., 2000.

Superior—The Complete History, by Thomas A. McPherson, Specialty Vehicle Press, 1995.

The Eureka Company—A Complete History, by Thomas A. McPherson, Specialty Vehicle Press, 1994.

Flxible Professional Vehicles—The Complete History, by Thomas A. McPherson, Specialty Vehicle Press, 1993.

TABLE OF CONTENTS:

DEDICATION

This book is respectfully dedicated to the generations of ambulance operators, drivers and attendants, first-aid volunteer rescue squad members, emergency medical technicians and paramedics who have saved, and prolonged, countless lives through their proficiency, competence, compassion and professionalism, and to the members of *The Professional Car Society* who have done so much to preserve and perpetuate the proud legacy of the classic passenger car-based ambulance, its antecedents and contemporary successors.

Acknowledgments

A compendium of this size and scope would not be possible without the assistance of many others who share the author's interest in North American ambulances and the companies that built them. We are sincerely grateful to the following individuals who shared their knowledge, resources and photos with us as we compiled this long-overdue history.

Close associate and longtime personal friend, **Thomas A. McPherson** again opened his voluminous photo collection to us. Tom has shared what is undoubtedly the largest and finest private collection of professional car photos and literature anywhere with all of us through the four superb books he has authored on the subject.

Without the "Two Steves," this book would be a lot thinner. **Steven B. Loftin** has been trading professional car photos with the author for more years than either of us cares to admit. A member of the sales team at American LaFrance/MedicMaster, Steve has been taking photos of ambulances and funeral cars since he was a teenager. EMT/Paramedic **Stephen Lichtman** has faithfully photographed all of the ambulances at Professional Car Society International Meets for many years. In addition to taking calendar-quality portraits of the cars, Steve painstakingly prepares a list of every vehicle in attendance for **The Professional Car**. **Ted Kalinowski** took

the photos which grave the covers of this book, and numerous others. Other PCS members we turned to for photos include PCS publicist **Gregg Merksamer**; **Tom Parkinson**; **Bernie DeWinter IV**, who is working on a comprehensive history of the Combination Coach; **Craig Stewart**; **Mike Riefer**; **Stan Ruff**; **Tony Karsnia**; **Jack Lister** and **Louis Farah**, Editor of **The California Collector**, the excellent newsletter of PCS' Southern California Chapter.

Special thanks to **James P. Martin**, Deputy Chief—EMS Command, Division 2, New York City Fire Department (FDNY) who provided us with photos of one of the EMS units of the type lost at the World Trade Center 9/11/01; FDNY historian **Jack Lerch**; Alan Craig, Director—Program Development, Metro Toronto Emergency Medical Services; **Len Langlois**, longtime owner/operator of the Chatham & District Ambulance Service; **Brandt Rosenbusch**, Curator for the Chrysler Historical Collection, and auto industry historian **John M. Conde**.

Thanks, too, to well-known fire apparatus photographers **Daniel Jasina**, **Steve Hagy** and **Dan Martin**, who took pictures of the ambulances as well as the fire engines; and automotive and fire apparatus historian/author **Matthew Lee**.

To any other contributors we may have inadvertently overlooked, our profound apologies.

Introduction

This book was published to fill a puzzling void in American motor vehicle reference literature. While many excellent books have been written about various other types of emergency vehicles—fire apparatus and heavy rescue trucks, police cars and even towing and recovery vehicles—no one, up to now, has published a book devoted exclusively to the development of the most noble of all motor vehicles—the life-saving ambulance.

As ironic as it may seem, for much of the past century ambulance production in the United States and Canada was an offshoot of the parent funeral car industry. In many communities, ambulance service was provided by the local undertaker. Hearses and ambulances utilized the same body shell, the basic purpose of which was to transport a recumbent person.

As the 1900s began, the horse-drawn ambulance had emerged as a distinct type of emergency vehicle. With the introduction of the first automobile ambulances at the end of the first decade of the new century, the pace of technological change accelerated dramatically, although basic ambulance body design did not. The tall, boxy ambulance body was replaced by the long, low limousine style in the mid-1920s. The next major advance was in the 1930s with the introduction of the long-wheelbase commercial chassis designed especially for the mounting of hearse and ambulance bodies designed and built by independent coachbuilders.

Most funeral car manufacturers offered two distinctly different types of ambulances. The Private Ambulance or Invalid Coach was intended primarily for patient transfer, while the emergency or "hospital type" ambulance was designed to get the patient to the hospital as quickly as possible while rendering first-aid en route. For nearly 60 years, one of the industry's staple products was the dual-purpose Combination Coach which could be used as either hearse or ambulance as required. The small-town undertaker thus needed only one special-purpose vehicle instead of two.

The zenith of the glamorous passenger car-based ambulance era was reached in the 1950s and 1960s when big Packard, Cadillac and Buick ambulances set the standard. But as attractively styled and smooth-riding as they were, passenger car-type ambulances lacked the interior space needed for increasingly advanced in-transit medical treatment. By the late 1960s a new generation of commercial vans were proving attractive alternatives to the expensive Cadillacs and Oldsmobiles.

Everything came to a head in the 1970s. New federal vehicle standards dictated interior dimensions, basic equipment carried, even the training of ambulance attendants. And the auto industry downsized its cars to comply with new fuel economy regulations. The effect on the old-line professional car manufacturers was devastating. The last passenger car-based ambulance was built in 1979.

Vastly roomier and more efficient van and modular-type ambulances took over entirely in the 1980s and remain the standard in the United States and Canada today. Major advances in emergency medicine and the arrival of highly-trained EMTs and Paramedics precipitated the transition from passenger car-based vehicles to van and modular-type ambulances.

Ambulances today come in all shapes and sizes. In addition to the universally used Types I, II and III, every imaginable type of vehicle has been adapted for first-responder service, ranging from all-terrain vehicles and sport utility vehicles to multi-million dollar medivac helicopters and jet air ambulances.

The focus of this book is the evolution of the automobile ambulance in North America and the companies, large and small, which built them. Not attempt has been made to similarly document the development of the equipment carried—stretchers, cots, backboards, resuscitators, oxygen systems, in-vehicle telemetry, etc., nor the life-saving practices so effectively used by their dedicated crews. These related subjects are worthy of books of their own.

From the beginning, American ambulances have been built on a wondrous variety of chassis. There was hardly a passenger car marque made that did not at one time or other bear ambulance coachwork. Several volumes this size wouldn't be enough to cover them all.

Although the cube-bodied, look-alike modular and van-type ambulances on the road today lack the pizzazz of the fondly-remembered passenger car type, they are far more efficient for both patients and crew. That's progress.

Walter M.P. McCall
Windsor, Ontario
June 2002

Rubber-tired ambulance with two-horse hitch, circa 1907. Note acetylene searchlight on roof. Mission Emergency Hospital, San Francisco, California.

The Horse-drawn Era

By popular definition, an **ambulance** is the conveyance used to transport the sick or injured to infirmary, hospital or other sanitary place where medical treatment is available. As a specialized means of transportation, the life-saving ambulance has been around in one form or another as long as the existence of emergency medicine.

The precise origin of what came to be known as the **emergency or hospital ambulance** is lost to time, but it would not be presumptuous to assume that hundreds—even thousands—of years ago the ill or injured were carried by family members or comrades on strong shoulders, or on some sort of crude litter or stretcher, from the home or place of illness, disease or injury to a quiet place where medical assistance, such as it was, could be rendered. Long before the word "ambulance" became part of our language, virtually every form of transportation known to man—from sledges and sleighs to beasts of burden, sedan chairs, oxcarts and farm wagons, had been pressed into service for this humanitarian purpose.

The medieval litter evolved into a covered stretcher, still lifted and carried by fleet-footed bearers. Next came the faster, more efficient wheeled cart, which was pushed or pulled by hand through the streets of village or town. The next advance—and it was a major one—was the much faster **horse-drawn** vehicle with two, then four, wheels.

The word "ambulance" is believed to have originated in France as a derivative of a Latin word—**ambulare**—which meant to move from one place to another. Because of the obvious need to transport large numbers of wounded soldiers, the word "ambulance" was closely associated with the military, to describe the mobile first-aid stations, which followed an army. The **"ambulances vo-lantes"** were "flying field hospitals" which followed Napoleon's armies across Europe in the early 1790s. Some 80 years later, the Red Cross emblem was first used as a symbol to identify field ambulances in the Franco-Prussian War.

The Civil War of 1860-1865 greatly accelerated the advancement of emergency medical treatment in the United States, as thousands of wounded and disabled soldiers were transported from the battlefields to infirmaries, hospitals and homes. The horse-drawn ambulance emerged as a distinct **type** of public service vehicle in America at about this time. It is generally believed that the first dedicated public ambulance service in the United States was established by a hospital in Cincinnati, Ohio, in 1866.

Three years later the Bellevue Hospital in New York City organized that city's first ambulance service. During the 1870s and 1880s, many communities across the country established hospital-based public ambulance services.

The first municipal or hospital ambulances were stark, boxy vehicles, which were typically drawn by a single horse. The driver sat out in the open. The narrow, unventilated rear compartment had room for one or two patient stretchers and a seat or stool for a doctor or medical attendant.

Roads were poor or non-existent. The suffering patient was often in for a rough ride as the ambulance lurched and jounced over rutted, muddy roads and unpaved streets. One can only wonder at the number of patients who worsened or expired due to injuries aggravated during the bone-jarring journey to infirmary or hospital.

By the late nineteenth century, two distinct **types** of ambulances had evolved in America. First was the **Hospital Ambulance**

7

which, as its name implied, was designed to transport the patient at the greatest possible speed to the hospital for emergency medical attention. The other was the non-emergency **Invalid or Private Ambulance,** which transferred the ill, or convalescent, at a more leisurely pace **to or from** the hospital or clinic.

At first, ambulance service was provided by local hospitals, asylums or by the municipal public health department. But as funeral directing evolved into a distinct profession, local undertakers began to provide ambulance service to their communities—a practice that continued well into the 20th century. The local undertaker was accustomed to assisting families at a time of crisis, and he was usually the only man in town who owned a vehicle in which a recumbent body—live or deceased—could be transported. In addition to his casket wagon or hearse, the progressive undertaker also offered his clientele an equally well-appointed ambulance or Invalid Carriage.

Horse-drawn vehicles of all types had become much more sophisticated by the final decade of the nineteenth century. Horse-drawn ambulances were standard items in the product catalogs of many carriage and wagon builders. Virtually all of America's hearse manufacturers also built ambulances. For much of the 20th century, in fact, the U.S. ambulance manufacturing industry was closely tied to the "parent" hearse industry.

The typical ambulance of the 1890s was a tall, rectangular vehicle with double rear doors. The driver sat in an open semi-cab where he could handle the horses (one or two) that pulled the vehicle. A gong or bell cleared the way through traffic as the ambulance went about its life-saving duties.

The interior was usually wood-paneled. On better grade vehicles, the cot or stretcher was suspended on straps, which hung from the ceiling, isolating the patient from at least some of the bumps and grinds. Ambulances were usually painted light colors—white, light gray or silver-gray. A Red Cross emblem was prominently displayed on its sides, or windows, to identify the wagon as an emergency vehicle.

Premium model ambulances featured at least one side-entrance door and a pair of elegant carriage lamps. Fine pinstriping and the owner or operator's name in block letters or script enhanced the vehicle's exterior appearance.

Horseless Ambulances

As the 1800s drew to a close, the first horseless carriages had sputtered uncertainly onto the scene. The noisy, notoriously unreliable automobile was regarded as little more than a passing fad, another plaything for the idle rich—certainly **never** as a replacement for the millions of horses which provided most of America's vehicular power.

Basic ambulance design changed remark-

Sayers & Scovill #60 horse-drawn side-entrance ambulance, circa 1900. Note two-tone gray exterior finish.

ably little during the first decade of the new century. The most significant improvement was the universal adoption of rubber tires, which cushioned the vehicle's ride and also significantly reduced noise levels on urban streets. Some luxury models even boasted electric lights.

Despite their undignified noise levels and less than 100 percent reliability, the far-sighted could already envision the day when the automobile would ultimately replace the horse. It is significant, therefore, that some of the first self-propelled vehicles actually placed into regular public service were life saving ambulances.

The first such vehicles were powered by batteries rather than the noisy internal combustion engine. Electric ambulances were providing clean, efficient, virtually silent service in a number of U.S. cities at the turn of the 19th century. The Michael Reese Hospital in Chicago had a battery-powered ambulance in service in 1899. Two New York City hospitals were using electric ambulances as early as 1900. St. Vincent's Hospital operated an electric ambulance built by F. R. Wood and Son of New York. The Lying-In Hospital of New York City placed an electric ambulance into service on April 1, 1900.

Style No. 192

AMBULANCE

BODY.... Is high-class construction, made of the very choicest air-dried lumber, ash being used entirely for framework and poplar for panels, and columns with all joints thoroughly imbedded in white lead, and panels glued on, screwed and plugged. There is a partition back of the driver's seat which has two drop sashes, and rear doors also have drop sashes in upper half so that ample ventilation can be had in hot weather. Glass lights at sides are 27 x 54 inches. Glass in sides, rear doors and front partition are all highly polished plate glass and beveled on edges. Inside of body in the clear on floor is 7 feet 1 inch long and 42 inches wide, but it has swelled sides which makes it 43½ inches wide above floor. Height is 5 feet. Body measures over all in length 11 feet 10 inches; in width, including columns, 4 feet 5 inches; height over all when set on gear is 8 feet 3 inches. Body is elevated 30 inches from floor. This body throughout is all that good material and workmanship can make.

EQUIPMENT. One complete Armleder Spiral Spring Ambulance Cot; elegant pair of fancy pattern long stem lamps entirely silver plated; two folding attendants' seats attached on right side of body; medicine chest attached to front partition; one nickel plated hand lantern suspended on a nickel plated bracket, with quick release spring attachment; 9-inch rotary fire department foot tread gong attached on front of foot panel, and a strongly supported step at rear end covered with corrugated rubber.

TRIMMINGS. Cushion, lazy back and seat fall are all finely upholstered with best quality leather. Curtains on partition back of driver's seat and on rear doors are mounted on metal spring rollers, and at side lights on silver plated stationary rods at top and bottom on which curtains slide. All curtains are fine quality silk. Heavy linoleum on inside floor and in front of driver's seat. Corrugated rubber for floor in front of driver's seat and on rear step. Rubber rain apron for front and rubber lamp covers. Heavy non-corrosive "never-wear-out" white metal point bands on hubs of wheels, pole tip and whiffletree ends. Silver plated dash rail, seat handle and whip socket. Spring lock on right door with heavy silver plated bar handles on outside and

inside. Left door is held secure by a spring catch with finger release lever. Pole hold back straps are heavy harness leather doubled and stitched.

GEAR.... Full platform, front truss has bent hounds and fancy finish. Slip pole, rowlock whiffletree fastenings and loop trace ferrules. Spring and axle couplings are coach box pattern. All parts of gear are closely fitted and smooth finished.

AXLES... Are best quality steel with double collar, coached shape, and have silver plated nuts. Front is 1¼-inch and rear, 1⅜-inch. Half Collinge or Timken Roller Bearing Axles are furnished when especially ordered, and then at an extra charge as named in price list.

WHEELS. Best quality second growth hickory with compressed banded hubs and concealed screws in rims at each side of spokes. (Patent wheels are furnished, if desired.) Spokes in front wheels are 1⅜-inch and in rear wheels 1½-inch. Front tires are 1¼ x ₁⁄₁₆ steel and rear 1⅜ x ₁⁄₁₆, projecting over rims and bolted between each and every spoke.

RUBBER TIRES. Are not furnished unless specially ordered, and then at an extra charge as given in price list.

SPRINGS. Are best oil-tempered steel and specially graded and proportioned to ride easy. Sides are 1¾-inch, 5 leaves, and cross, 1¾-inch, 6 leaves.

BRAKE.... Is not furnished unless specially ordered, and then at an extra charge as given in price list.

PAINTING. Is strictly first class in every way and high-class coach finish. We will paint it any colors desired except white or silver gray without extra charge. Extra charge for white or silver gray is given in price list. We make no extra charge for engraving initial on glass at sides of seat, Red Cross sign on side glass lights, or for lettering name in gold leaf, or, if preferred, we furnish metal name plates.

APPROXIMATE WEIGHT, including regular equipment, 1,450 pounds.

Advertising cut for Premium horse-drawn ambulance built by the O. Armleder Company, Cincinnati, Ohio.

An electric ambulance also earned a dubious place in history. The mortally wounded President William McKinley was rushed to a hospital in Buffalo, New York, in a Wood Electric ambulance after he was felled by an assassin's bullet in September 1901. He died eight days later.

Mount Sinai Hospital in New York City also had an electric ambulance in service in 1904. By 1906, no fewer than five battery-powered ambulances were quietly plying the streets of New York on their missions of mercy. Cleveland, Ohio's Lakeside Hospital offered its patients the services of an electric ambulance in 1905, and Indianapolis, Indiana, placed a dual-purpose Waverly Electric Combination Ambulance and Police Patrol into service in 1906.

In its issue of November 9, 1907, **_The Scientific American_** published descriptions and illustrations of two automobile ambu-lances, one on a Rapid motor truck chassis (originally the Grabowsky, a precursor to the GMC truck), and the other a large White Steamer Ambulance being evaluated at the time by the U.S. Army. Loaded with a ton of medical supplies, the 18-horsepower White Steamer made a 300-mile proving trip from Washington, D.C., to Gretna, Pennsylvania, at an average speed of 17 miles an hour.

The Wood Electric Ambulance had a useful operating range of 25 to 30 miles. A pair of two-horsepower motors mounted on the rear axle propelled the 4,000-pound vehicle. Current was supplied by 44 storage batteries. A controller under the driver's seat permitted forward speeds of six, nine and 13 miles an hour, and two reverse speeds—three and six miles an hour.

"There are many reasons why an automobile ambulance has marked advantages over the horse-drawn vehicle," an article in

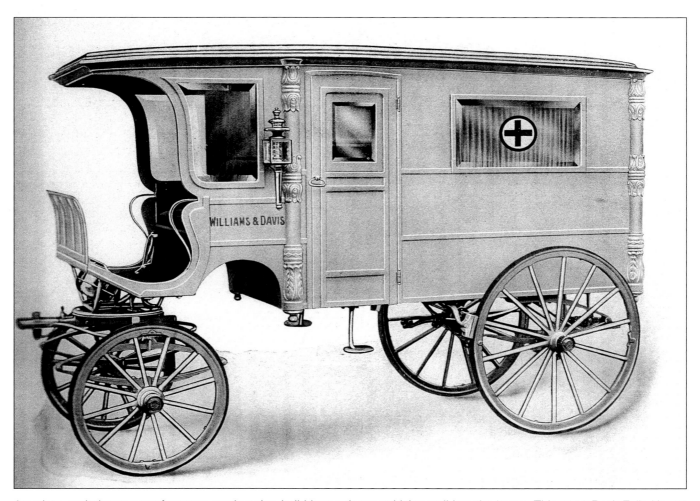

American ambulance manufacturers continued to build horse-drawn vehicles well into the 'teens. This 1913 Rock Falls No. 33 Side-Door Ambulance came factory-wired for electric lights.

The Scientific American noted in March 1910. "It is capable of greater sustained speed, and when the destination is reached no care has to be paid to the steaming horse, and both surgeon and driver can devote their attention to the injured person. Accidents in ambulances are of frequent occurrence owing to their speed and right of way, but electric vehicles can be stopped in their own length. Every second is of importance to an injured person, and speed and ease of riding will undoubtedly soon make them a great favorite among hospital authorities."

"Another feature of interest is the lower cost of maintenance. An ambulance is usually idle twenty or more hours out of the twenty-four, and this gives ample time for charging the batteries. There is no time lost in hitching up, and the stable may be in the hospital proper, without the dangers of stable odors," the magazine stated.

The interior of the Wood Electric Ambulance was trimmed in premium leather. The patient stretcher, or bed, slid out the rear of the vehicle "...being caught by irons, stands out parallel with the sidewalk, thus enabling a patient to be placed upon the bed without the necessity of being jolted, which is inseparable to the use of stationary beds."

In summary, then, the horse-drawn ambulance changed relatively little over the two-decade span between 1890 and 1910. Following is a description of the state-of-the-art "Type 33 Two-Horse Hitch Side-Door Ambulance" offered by the Rock Falls Manufacturing Co. of Rock Falls, Illinois, at the close of the first decade of the new century:

Body—Glass at driver's seat, four fine hand-carved columns, two on each side with drops; body nicely molded, double rear doors with drop sash; curved leather dash, ceiled inside, closed behind driver's seat, with sliding sash; one door on left-hand side with imitation door and step on opposite side; stationary rear step. Inside length back of seat about seven feet, eight inches; inside width about three feet, three inches, inside height about five feet, three inches. Polished beveled plate glass throughout.

Outside Trimmings—Silver-plated pole crab, single tree tips, hub bands, seat rails and door handles; suitable side lamps with silver heads and tails; leather cushion; rubber to mat; seat fully upholstered in leather. Our special doorstops hold doors in any position.

Ambulance Arrangement—Fitted regularly with our Patent Ambulance Chair swung from the ceiling. Can also furnish, if preferred, with upholstered cot, wood or rattan, on rollers with handholds for carrying and swung from ceiling by coil springs

The first self-propelled American ambulances were turn-of-the-century electrics. This virtually silent "side-loader" served Lying-in Hospital of New York, 1900.

and straps in guides to prevent side motion. Side seats in one or two sections made to fold down close to sides and upholstered in tan leather. Inside drawers for medicine, instruments and bandages slide under driver's seat. Speaking tube for driver.

Curtains—Shirred curtains on rods for large side windows, spring roller curtains for other windows. All curtains made from best quality gray broadcloth.

Painting—Finished regularly in gray, no striping, but can be painted any color and striped as desired, also lettered in gold leaf. Silver or polished brass name plates extra, according to size and amount of lettering. Finished in natural wood coloring on inside.

This ambulance is furnished regularly with lamp covers, storm aprons, pole and stay straps. These ambulances are all wired for electric lights while being built and lights can be added at any time at additional cost. The style, quality, workmanship and finish are strictly high grade, and it makes a fine vehicle for undertakers' use.

The Rock Falls Ambulance rode on 1 1/2-inch thick solid rubber tires. Brakes were $25 extra.

As the first decade of the new century came to a close, the horseless carriage had made astounding progress. No longer a trouble-prone plaything, the automobile was dramatically changing the face of the nation. In 1900, there were only a handful of struggling automobile manufacturers in America.

But by 1910, what began as an offshoot of the bicycle industry, had already developed into a major new industry. Among the dozens of players in the burgeoning motor vehicle industry were such recognized names as Oldsmobile, Ford, Packard, Cadillac, Pierce-Arrow, Winton and dozens of others.

If the ultra-conservative undertaker could see the advantages afforded by the automobile hearse, then the *motorized ambulance* could not be far behind. Small numbers of battery and steam-powered vehicles had proved beyond a doubt the practicality and superiority of the self-propelled hospital ambulance. Now the time had come for the next major advance in vehicle technology.

Exactly who was the first to place a *gasoline-propelled* motor ambulance into service

in America, *where* it was used and precisely *when* is not recorded. It is likely, however, that sometime prior to 1909 an undertaker or hospital administrator with mechanical inclination had a formerly horse-drawn ambulance body transferred onto an automobile chassis.

What *is* known is that the first *factory designed and built* automobile ambulance commercially marketed in the United States was introduced in 1909. This pioneering vehicle was designed and built by the James Cunningham, Son & Company of Rochester, New York. Founded in 1838, James Cunningham, Son & Co. was one of America's largest and most respected old-line carriage builders. Cunningham was internationally known for its elegant landaus, broughams and other fine carriages built for generations of America's wealthy families. This company was also the nation's leading builder of premium grade horse-drawn hearses, casket wagons and ambulances.

With sales of horse-drawn carriages already sharply declining with enthusiastic acceptance of the automobile, Cunningham had introduced its first motor-driven passenger car in 1908. It was only a matter of months before the company mounted one of its high-grade ambulance bodies on its own superbly engineered automobile chassis.

Announced in the leading funeral service trade journals in April 1909, the Cunningham *Model 774 Auto Ambulance* was powered by a 32-horsepower, four-cylinder engine of proprietary manufacture and rode on pneumatic tires. The modern Cunningham ambulance body was equipped with electric lighting, a suspended cot, two attendant seats and a side-mounted gong.

As with most vehicles of the early motor era, the driver or chauffeur sat in a wide-open cab.

Two months later, one of Cunningham's principal competitors in the U.S. hearse and ambulance industry—the Crane & Breed Mfg. Co. of Cincinnati, Ohio—introduced America's first factory-built motor hearse, which was followed in little over a year by Crane & Breed's own Auto Ambulance.

The Cunningham Auto Ambulance was well received by the undertaking trade. The age of the speedy automobile ambulance had arrived!

Warning Devices

Because of relatively light traffic patterns of the day, horse-drawn ambulances didn't need much in the way of audible or visual warning devices to clear their way through traffic. The word "Ambulance" prominently painted on the sides of the vehicle, or on a forward-facing signboard, was enough to clearly identify the horse-drawn ambulance or Invalid Carriage as an emergency vehicle. A distinctive exterior color—white, light gray or silver gray—with prominent Red Cross emblems also provided visual separation from the other horse-drawn vehicles on the road.

In cities and larger towns, hospital or emergency-type ambulances were usually equipped with a bell or gong mounted at the front of the vehicle within easy reach of the driver or attendant. On deluxe-type ambulances, a rotary-type gong was mounted under the driver's footboard, actuated by a foot-operated button.

James Cunningham, Son & Company introduced the first commercially produced gasoline-powered auto ambulance in the United States in 1909. Model 774 was powered by a 32-horsepower four-cylinder engine.

Cunningham Auto Ambulances operated by Rochester, New York General Hospital, circa 1913. Note warning gongs, "ambulance" signs above windshields.

Early motor ambulance on Haynes chassis, body builder unknown. Note open semi-type cab, acetylene headlamps.

The Motor Era Begins
1910 - 1919

The American automobile industry entered a period of spectacular growth and technological advance during the second decade of the new century. By the end of the teens—thanks largely to Henry Ford and his universal Model "T"—the automobile had evolved from an expensive indulgence for the well-to-do to a viable, dependable and, most importantly, an **affordable** alternative to the horse and buggy for millions of Americans. The newfangled automobile provided heretofore undreamed of freedom and mobility for all, regardless of social status. No other invention had so thoroughly transformed the face of the nation.

This social revolution didn't involve just passenger vehicles. Almost overnight the snorting, clanking motor truck rendered the horse-drawn dray obsolete. Virtually every other type of vehicular transportation, from omnibuses to fire engines and funeral cars, was similarly affected. So it was that, by the end of the teeming teens, the horse-drawn **ambulance** had already become something of a rarity.

The gasoline-powered automobile ambulance had arrived on the scene in 1909. The first commercially marketed motor ambulances and hearses had been introduced by the James Cunningham, Son & Co. of Rochester, New York, and the Crane & Breed Mfg. Co. of Cincinnati, Ohio, that year. Within a year several other hearse and ambulance manufacturers had also added motor–driven professional cars to their product lines—while astutely maintaining production of horse-drawn vehicles while there was still market demand for them.

The new automobile hearses and ambulances were far more expensive than horse-drawn vehicles, typically costing several times the price of a new horse-drawn equipage. Early sales were, consequently, limited to a few large, prosperous funeral directing firms, hospitals and ambulance operators in the bigger cities. Many otherwise progressive-minded undertakers and hospital boards, however, still had serious reservations about the dependability of these vehicles.

For one thing, except for professional chauffeurs, few people knew how to drive an automobile, so special training was required for driver-mechanics. As the passenger car and motor truck displaced the horse and the cost of motor vehicles of all types continued to fall as a result of high-volume vehicle production and the resulting economies of scale, the gasoline-powered ambulance became the norm rather than the exception to the rule.

Once given careful consideration, the new auto ambulance clearly offered major advantages over the horse-drawn type. The high initial purchase price was offset by substantially lower operating and maintenance costs over the long run. With an auto ambulance there were no horses to stable, feed and care for. Horses ate hay 24 hours a day: the motor-propelled ambulance incurred operating expense only when it was actually running. Gasoline was relatively inexpensive and, with the exploding popularity of the pleasure car, was now widely available.

The auto ambulance had a virtually unlimited range of operation. Horses tired on long runs—especially when galloping to the scene of an accident and then back to the hospital. One motor ambulance could easily do the work of several horse-drawn vehicles. Above all, the auto ambulance could operate at sustained high speed—a prime requisite for any emergency vehicle. For these reasons, the vastly more efficient automobile ambulance quickly overtook, and replaced, horse-drawn rigs.

With the arrival of much more refined and dependable motor equipment, the electric ambulance, which had showed such promise early in the century all but disappeared, as did steam-powered ambulances. The superiority of the internal-combustion gasoline engine over all other types of propulsion had been proved beyond all reasonable doubt.

As the new century entered its second decade, ambulance service in America was still being primarily provided by local hospitals, the municipal department of health and, increasingly, by the neighborhood funeral director. Funeral homes had staff on call around the clock and on-site garages in which they housed and maintained their professional vehicles—hearses, casket wagons, pallbearers' coaches—and a well-equipped public ambulance.

The undertaker usually provided ambulance service to the community on a goodwill basis—but the undertaker's ambulance was also a subtle and highly effective means of advertising for his business. In addition to emergency service, the undertaker's ambulance was available to transfer the ill and convalescent to or from the local hospital, infirmary or clinic.

Riddle Carriage & Hearse Company of Ravenna, Ohio built this ambulance on a 1913 White chassis for St. Laurence Hospital. White-coated attendant gives directions to uniformed chauffeur.

Formerly horse-drawn Crane & Breed ambulance body remounted on a 1914 Cadillac "Thirty" chassis. Operated by Henderson Undertakers, location unknown.

Crane & Breed mounted hearse and ambulance bodies on expensive Winton Six chassis. Crane & Breed/Winton Model 1127 "Colonial Limousine Style Ambulance" was built in 1913.

Typical "Private Ambulance" on four-cylinder White chassis operated by House of Lanyon Undertakers, Chicago, 1913. Note fully enclosed cab.

Kings County New York Department of Public Charities operated this White Steamer ambulance, circa 1910.

Early automobile ambulances—at least most of those produced before the First World War—didn't look a whole lot different from their horse-drawn predecessors. Bodies still were tall and narrow with double doors at the rear. Most had at least one side door. The driver still sat out in the open, his only protection from the elements a two-piece, folding glass windshield. A blanket or lap robe was still a necessity in the winter months. On some models a waterproof storm apron buttoned into place in the event of rain.

The well-dressed ambulance still sported a pair of elegant carriage lamps, and the owner/operators' initials were sometimes etched into the side window glass of the rudimentary "C"-type cab.

As the motor era evolved, there were still two distinct **types** of ambulances in general service in the United States and Canada. First was the **Emergency or Hospital Ambulance** with its white-uniformed driver and attendant and traffic-clearing gong or bell. The other was the non-emergency **Invalid Carriage** or **Private Ambulance,** which quietly transferred patients from home to, or from, the hospital or medical center. Emergency ambulances were usually painted white, gray or silver with a prominent Red Cross emblem in the windows. The Invalid Ambulance, on the other hand, could be almost any color such as maroon or dark blue or green, always with tasteful pinstriping or lettering on the sides. Some vehicles were two-toned, with one color used on the body and another contrasting color on the fenders, aprons and wheels.

The rear compartment was wood-paneled or, on premium models, upholstered in fine leather. The modern ambulance of 1912 had rear compartment ventilation, electric lighting and a seat for the attending physician or a medical attendant. The cot, or folding chair/cot, was suspended from the ceiling. One or two additional stretchers could be carried if necessary. The attendant communicated with the driver via a speaking tube. Eye-catching appearance was important: the ambulance was more than a symbol of mercy to the public—it was also a rolling billboard for its operator.

The first factory-built automobile ambulances (and hearses) were mounted on motor chassis designed and assembled by their makers. The James Cunningham, Son & Co. was an old-line carriage builder which had built its first passenger car for its well-heeled "carriage trade" customers in 1908. By contrast, rival Crane & Breed was **not** exclusively a vehicle maker. The Cincinnati, Ohio, company was a prominent casket manufacturer and national undertakers' supply house. In addition to coffins, caskets and burial cases, Crane & Breed offered a complete range of funeral directors supplies, including hearses, ambulances, casket wagons and embalmers' buggies.

Four-cylinder engines of proprietary manufacture powered the first Cunningham and Crane & Breed auto ambulances and

York-Hoover ambulance body on a 1918 Cadillac Type 57 chassis. Introduced in 1915, the Cadillac V-8 made this make a favorite with hearse and ambulance builders. Note Klaxon horn.

motor hearses. Cunningham began making its own superbly engineered motors in 1910. Crane & Breed, meanwhile, entered into a long and successful partnership with one of America's oldest automobile companies, the Winton Motor Car Company of Cleveland, Ohio. Crane & Breed would mount its exquisitely crafted ambulance and hearse bodies on the expensive six-cylinder Winton chassis (which vigorously competed with the famous "three Ps"—Peerless, Packard and Pierce-Arrow) into the 1920s.

By 1913, Crane & Breed was marketing its impressive Model 1127 "Colonial Limousine Ambulance" with open semi-cab and beveled glass windows on the prestigious Winton Six chassis.

Another early automobile chassis favored by hearse and ambulance manufacturers was the big (and expensive) White Steamer,

which was built and marketed by the White Company of Cleveland, Ohio. Like the electrics it competed with, the White Steamer boasted extremely quiet, clean operation—important considerations for ambulance operators and funeral directors. Some of the first funeral car and ambulance bodies mounted on automobile chassis were Whites. As the teens progressed, White offered a very popular four-cylinder light duty truck chassis which found much favor with specialty body builders, including the hearse and ambulance industry.

The F. F. Roberts Co. of Chicago conducted one of that city's first automobile funerals using a White-chassised hearse in 1909, and the first automobile funeral conducted in New York City, in 1910, was led by a White steamer outfitted with a Cunningham carved hearse body. Soon, however, the internal-combustion gasoline engine had eclipsed the steamer, too.

Hundreds of military ambulances with simple wooden bodies were shipped to the U.S. Army overseas during World War I. This is a typical World War I Red Cross ambulance on a Model "T" Ford chassis.

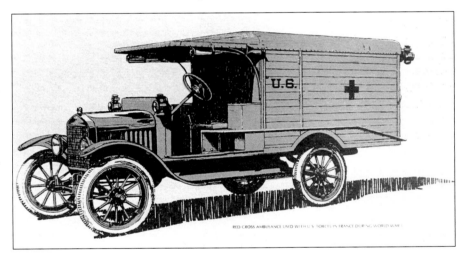

Impressive fleet of Cunningham limousine ambulances operated by Smith & Smith Undertakers of Newark, New Jersey, circa 1919.

Other early automobile and light commercial chassis fitted with hearse and ambulance coachwork included the air-cooled "Knox Waterless" built by the Knox Automobile Company of Springfield, Massachusetts, and the Autocar, the latter a buckboard style truck, built by the Autocar Company in Ardmore, Pennsylvania.

Another old-line hearse builder—Sayers & Scovill, also of Cincinnati—entered the emerging motor hearse and ambulance field in 1912. Incorporated in 1876, the Sayers & Scovill Company was a well-known and respected carriage builder. The company had added horse-drawn hearses and ambulances to its product line in 1872. Like its rivals, Sayers & Scovill's first auto hearses and ambulances were assembled vehicles, which used proprietary powerplants. In 1914, S&S offered the trade the dual-purpose Sayers & Scovill Pallbearers' Coach which, by removal of the right front seat, could be configured to carry a standard ambulance cot. Such vehicles, separate from the emergency-type ambulance, were referred to as **Combinations**, or **Invalid Carriages.**

Other early builders of motorized ambulances and funeral cars included the United States Carriage Company of Columbus, Ohio, which marketed its professional cars under the Great Eagle name; the Kunkel Funeral Car Company of Galion, Ohio; the Riddle Hearse & Carriage Co. of Ravenna, Ohio; and the Rock Falls Manufacturing Company of Rock Falls, Illinois. Another luxury car maker, the Peerless Automobile Co. of Cleveland, also marketed motor ambulances under its own name.

Two companies destined to play major roles in the American hearse and ambulance business were incorporated in the teens.

The colorful and charismatic Maurice Wolfe established the Meteor Motor Car Company in Piqua, Ohio. Wolfe entered the auto industry in its infancy in 1901 as a mechanic and salesman. Like other auto industry pioneers, Wolfe yearned to own and run his own automobile company, so in 1913 he purchased the struggling Clark Motor Car Company of Shelbyville, Indiana. Wolfe relocated the business to Piqua, Ohio, and renamed it the Meteor Motor Car Company. The new company's first products were a line of sturdily built carved-panel hearses mounted on Wolfe's own assembled chassis. Within a very short time, Wolfe had added automobile ambulances to Meteor's well-received product line.

At first, Wolfe purchased bodies for his professional cars from the A. J. Miller Company of Bellefontaine, Ohio, an arrangement that remained in place for about three years. In 1917, A. J. Miller started building and marketing hearses and ambulances on its own and soon became one of Meteor's principal competitors. Ironically, these two companies merged four decades later. The first Meteor hearses and ambulances were built in 1914. In addition to hearses and straight ambulances, Meteor also marketed large pallbearers' sedans, which could do dual duty as Invalid Cars or ambulances.

Another one of America's best-remembered hearse and ambulance builders entered the professional car field at about this time. Established in Cedarville, Iowa, in 1868, the Henney Buggy Company eventually relocated to Freeport, Illinois. Once one of the largest buggy makers in the world, Henney watched its business wither away under the onslaught of the automobile. By the early teens, the writing was on the wall. If it was to survive, the company had to find something else to produce.

The Henney Buggy Company had a large, highly skilled workforce of woodworkers and carvers. The company's salvation was the manufacture of funeral cars with richly carved wood imitation drapery panels. John W. Henney & Company was established in Freeport in 1916. As with other hearse makers, it wasn't long before Henney had added ambulances to its product range as a profitable sideline to its core funeral car business. Later renamed the Henney Motor Company, this company went on to eventually become the industry's acknowledged leader and style-setter.

A similar transitory tale was unfolding over in Rock Falls, Illinois, where The Eureka Company also watched with alarm as its buggy business shriveled up and died. Like Henney, Eureka employed talented woodcarvers who switched from making buggies to carved-panel hearse bodies as a means of survival.

By 1918, Eureka had become one of a number of specialized motor hearse and ambulance builders which had sprung up around the country.

Then came the First World War. In 1917 and 1918, American companies large and small joined the war effort, producing all manner of war materials for America's fighting forces overseas. The war saw unprecedented demand for motor vehicles of all kinds—including thousands of army ambulances. Many hearse and ambulance builders in the U.S. were awarded contracts to build utilitarian military ambulance bodies, which were mounted on extended light passenger car chassis such as the Model "T" Ford and Dodge Bros.

These utilitarian *field ambulances* bore almost no resemblance to their civilian cousins. The U.S. Army ambulance had a platform-type body with low sides and roll-down canvas sides. Designed to operate over rough terrain, their principal purpose was the speedy evacuation of injured soldiers from the blood-soaked battlefields of France. These military ambulances were painted olive drab or khaki with unmistakable ambulance markings—a prominent Red Cross on a white background. These rugged military ambulances served with distinction on the Western Front, fulfilling the same humanitarian role as the "*ambulance volante*" units had in France more than 120 years earlier.

The "Great War" was followed by a period of euphoria and economic prosperity. Auto-mobile manufacturers were doing a booming business. During this extremely eventful decade, the auto industry had reached maturity. The Ford Motor Company had sold millions of its Model "T"s. General Motors was a highly successful combination of a number of auto companies—Chevrolet, Buick, Oldsmobile, Oakland and Cadillac—under a single banner. Hundreds of independents—Studebaker, Hudson and Packard among them—were also thriving.

By the close of the second decade of the 20th century, the automobile ambulance had advanced with public hygiene and the evolving science of emergency medicine. The post-World War I ambulance had a fully enclosed cab, electric lighting inside and out and a much improved ride for both patient and attendants. A bell or a small wind machine called a **siren horn** cleared the way through urban traffic and lustily announced the lifesaving ambulance's arrival.

The impressive advances of the tumultuous teens, however, would pale in comparison to the progress of the Roaring Twenties. As the decade closed, the horse-drawn ambulance had become an anachronism.

The "Roaring Twenties" marked yet another decade of astonishing growth and progress for the American automobile industry—and, similarly, for the highly specialized hearse and ambulance industry.

Warning Devices

The arrival of the automobile, explosive growth in the nation's motor vehicle population and vastly improved roads with their resulting traffic congestion created a real need to "see and **be** seen." When the decade began, the vast majority of the ambulances being used in America were still horse-drawn. As the decade ended, the speedy automobile ambulance had all but taken over—at least where emergency ambulances were concerned. Horse-drawn ambulances and Invalid Carriages could still be found in many smaller communities.

Most motor ambulances of this era were equipped with a manually operated bell or gong. A forward-facing "Ambulance" sign was usually mounted on the cab roof above the windshield. Like most passenger cars, automobile ambulances were also equipped with a hand-operated, bulb-type horn or an electrically powered Klaxon. A single red-lens light—sometimes bearing a Red Cross emblem—might be affixed to the front of the vehicle.

A new type of warning device—the electric **siren horn**—had also recently made its appearance. Initially, these were more commonly found on fire engines and police motorcycles than they were on ambulances. Their rising and falling wailing sound was considered distressing to the patients carried therein—but not for long.

Luxurious 1920 Cunningham Model 66-A Ambulance on V5 chassis. Note polished metal hood and disc wheels.

1929 Flxible-Buick ambulance for U.S. Army Medical Dept., assigned to Selfridge Field near Detroit. Flxible Company had a long and successful partnership with Buick Motor Division of General Motors.

Toward a Mature Industry 1920 - 1929

By 1920, the horse-drawn ambulance had largely disappeared from the streets of larger cities and towns. Yes, horse-drawn invalid wagons could still be found in smaller communities where they routinely transported patients to and from the hospital on a non-emergency basis, but for life-saving emergency service, the speedy, reliable automobile ambulance had all but replaced Old Dobbin.

While local hospitals and municipal health departments continued to provide ambulance service to their communities, more often than not this essential public service was now being rendered by local funeral homes. In addition to his big, black carved-panel hearse, the undertaker's garage more often than not also housed a Private Ambulance or Invalid Car, which was available to the general public.

The up-to-date auto ambulance of 1920 would bear little resemblance to those being produced by the end of the decade. The "War To End All Wars" had ended in 1918, but a period of postwar prosperity was followed by a serious recession in the early 1920s.

The standard automobile ambulance of 1920 was still a tall, narrow-bodied vehicle that rode on wood-spoked wheels. As the 1920s began, there were still two distinct *types* of ambulances in general service—the emergency or hospital ambulance, and the aptly-named Invalid Car.

Following is a description of an Invalid Car which was placed into service by the Paxson Undertaking Company of Springfield, Missouri, in 1923. This glowing description was published in a leading funeral service trade journal of the day:

"A recent addition to the equipment of the company is the *Invalids Car.* It is the most complete car of its kind in the state and the only one equipped with hot and cold water. This car has an air mattress on a Bomgardner cot, lung-motor, baby basket, electric fan, built-in cabinets for linens and surgical supplies, a first-aid kit and an emergency cabinet with every appliance likely to be needed in a sick room. It might almost be called *a hospital on wheels.*"

"It is a car of beautiful coloring...white with trimmings of maroon. On the side it bears the slogan of the company... 'Where Service Means More Than A Mere Word.' This great Invalid Car has truly been the talk of the town since it was purchased a short time ago."

Even though the equipment carried would indicate that this vehicle was used both as an Invalid Car *and* as an emergency ambulance, it did not quite fit the definition of the dual-purpose *Combination Hearse/Ambulance,* which would appear on the scene a little later. Through the teens and 1920s, the term "Combination" was commonly applied to two different types of vehicles—the undertaker's large pallbearers' sedan or family limousine which could be quickly and easily reconfigured to carry an ambulance cot for use as an ambulance or Invalid Car, or the dual-purpose Combination Casket Wagon and Ambulance. The latter was a plain-sided, panel-type vehicle used to transport caskets from the funeral home or railway station. In a pinch this vehicle could be used as an ambulance. A Red Cross insignia was inserted into its small side windows for this purpose.

There was still a distinct line between a processional hearse and a patient-carrying ambulance. However, that line began to blur somewhat during the 1920s. The most significant development in U.S. hearse and ambulance design during the 1920s was the sudden emergence of the **limousine style** professional car during the first half of the decade.

For most of the previous three decades, the prototypical American hearse was of the eight- or twelve-column style with carved wooden drapery panels between the columns. Later models sometimes substituted plate glass in the center windows, or glass all around. It was this gloomy, carved panel hearse that had made the transition from horse to motor power. Although a few limousine style vehicles were used by undertakers as both hearses and, especially, as ambulances during the teens, the typical hearse of 1920 was still of the carved, columned style which had dominated the industry since the 1890s.

It would appear that The Eureka Company of Rock Falls, Illinois, was the first hearse and ambulance manufacturer to champion the limousine body style, in about 1922. The limousine funeral car was designed to look just like the finest passenger cars of the day. With its long, low lines and large glass area above the body belt line, the limousine style hearse was intended to blend in harmoniously with the passenger cars in the funeral procession. The earlier carved style hearse towered above the other cars and was unmistakably the focal point of the funeral procession.

So well did the sleek, new limousine style hearse blend into the funeral cortege that a new name was minted to identify

Big undertakers' limousines often did double-duty. Combination pallbearers' coach and ambulance built by Dominion Manufacturers, Toronto, Canada, 1922.

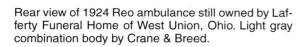

Rear view of 1924 Reo ambulance still owned by Lafferty Funeral Home of West Union, Ohio. Light gray combination body by Crane & Breed.

it—**Funeral Coach.** From this point on, the limousine style hearse had a "Funeral Coach" nameplate mounted in its windshield to unmistakably impart the vehicle's function.

Eureka precipitated a styling revolution in the U.S. professional car industry. Within a year or two, virtually every hearse and ambulance maker in America offered its customers the trendy, new limousine style vehicles. The carved-panel hearse was suddenly woefully out-of-date.

Ambulance operators, public and private, received the new limousine body style with equal enthusiasm. The smart, new Limousine Ambulance sported long, low lines. The large side windows let in plenty of light. For privacy, the rear side windows were fitted with frosted or ornamental leaded glass, often with a Red Cross motif. The rear side doors were equipped with pull-down window blinds for privacy for the patient. To subtly state its purpose, the limousine ambulance of the mid- to late-1920s had an "Ambulance" or "Invalid Coach" nameplate mounted behind the windshield glass.

Almost without exception, ambulance production in the United States and Canada was an offshoot of the "parent" funeral car industry. With the introduction of the new limousine style, the same basic body shell could now be used for **both** vehicles—the limousine funeral coach **and** the emergency or invalid-type ambulance. This would be the industry standard for the next 60 years.

Like the auto industry, the professional car industry reached maturity during the 1920s. There were many milestone corporate developments, too. The industry's principal players still included such long-established firms as Sayers & Scovill and Cunningham. Crane & Breed (which, with Cunningham, had pioneered the auto hearse and ambulance) built its last Winton-chassised professional cars in 1923. Other firms which had switched from buggy and wagon making to hearses and ambulances as a means of survival were prospering—Meteor, Henney, A. J. Miller and Eureka. Meanwhile, several other once well known builders fell by the wayside—Kunkel, Hoover, Rock Falls and Riddle among them.

Two major new players entered the burgeoning hearse and ambulance business in the mid-1920s. The Superior Body Company of Lima, Ohio, and The Flxible Company of Loudonville, Ohio, were already successful bus body builders. Founded in 1914, Flxible had switched from making motorcycle sidecars to Buick-chassised buses in the early 1920s. Founded in 1923, Superior made bus bodies for mounting on the locally built Garford truck chassis. Both of these companies added funeral coaches and ambulances to their product lines at about the same time, in 1925.

Structurally, there was little difference between a wood-framed bus body and the

Most aristocratic of all ambulance body styles was formal open-front Town Car. The Eureka Company built this classic Town Car Ambulance on a 1929 Lincoln chassis for the Balbirnie Funeral Home of Muskegon, Michigan.

SHOWING CANOPY OVER DRIVER'S SEAT

DESIGNED AND BUILT BY
THE EUREKA COMPANY
ROCK FALLS, ILLINOIS

smaller limousine-type hearse or ambulance body. Production materials, methods and tooling were virtually identical.

The Flxible Company introduced its first Buick-based funeral cars and ambulances in 1925. The close relationship between Flxible and the Buick Motor Division of General Motors would continue for many years. Superior's first ambulances and hearses were built on lengthened Cadillac V8 chassis, but within two years Superior had switched over to Studebaker chassis. The Studebaker Corporation became a major advertiser in funeral service trade journals. Although Superior mounted its limousine style ambulance and hearse bodies on extended Studebaker chassis, these vehicles were advertised as "Studebaker Equipment" and the Superior Body Company name was nowhere to be found in Studebaker's often lavish trade journal advertising.

The John W. Henney Company of Freeport, Illinois, was also doing very well. The company had earned an enviable reputa-

tion for quality and innovation. The first Henney hearses and ambulances were built on assembled chassis. Henney purchased components—Continental engines, Borg & Beck clutches, Timken axles, etc.—from independent suppliers and assembled its own chassis in the Freeport plant. Henney also built moderately priced hearses and ambulances on the Velie chassis.

The most unique ambulance offered by this company in the 1920s was the **Henney Air Ambulance**. Built by the Great Lakes Aircraft Corp., the Henney Air Ambulance carried a crew of four—pilot, co-pilot and two medical attendants—and the patient who, no doubt, was whisked to and from the airport in a modern Henney-built ambulance. Few (if any) were actually sold.

James Cunningham, Son & Co. of Rochester, New York, continued to service the carriage trade with very expensive hearses and ambulances built on the company's own chassis. The most interesting ambulance turned out by this firm during the 1920s was a fully armored ambulance designed and custom-built for the firm of J. T. Hinton & Sons of Memphis, Tennessee.

The Meteor Motor Car Company introduced a companion line of smaller, lower-priced hearses, ambulances and funeral service cars, which it marketed as the **Mort** line. Like rival A. J. Miller, Meteor sold its products direct from the factory, with no salesmen or field representatives to add to overhead. Meteor continued to use its own assembled chassis, while rival A. J. Miller mounted its limousine hearse and ambulance bodies on Nash, Packard and Cadillac chassis.

The Cadillac Motor Car Division of General Motors—which had actively promoted its V8 chassis to hearse and ambulance builders as well as to other commercial vehicle users in the late teens and early twenties—entered the ever-expanding hearse and ambulance

Interior view of Cunningham auto ambulance, early 1920s. Note suspended Bomgardner cot, army-type canvas stretcher on floor and leaded rear side windows.

business *on its own* for several years in the late 1920s. Limousine style bodies for Cadillac's premium-grade "Custom-Built" Funeral Coaches and Ambulances, however, were built for Cadillac by Meteor.

Sayers & Scovill bestowed some colorful names on its ambulance models of this era. The company entered the decade with the S&S Samaritan Sedan/Ambulance—a big combination pallbearers' coach and ambulance. The company's first limousine style ambulance, introduced in 1921, was named the Sayers & Scovill Kensington, an S&S ambulance model designation, which would continue for the next four decades. By the end of the decade two other S&S ambulance

models—the Evanston and Fairmont, had joined the Kensington. These luxurious professional cars reflected the end of a dizzying period of prosperity and ostentation which would soon come crashing down with the devastating stock market crash of October 1929.

Hard times—*very* hard times—lay just around the corner.

Custom-built 1927 Packard 633 ambulance for the U.S. Department of Commerce. Detroit Fire Department received an identical Packard. Bodywork believed to be by Dietrich.

Ambulances and hearses lined up to receive victims of a Chicago mine disaster, mid-1920s. Big car at left is a Meteor ambulance.

Warning Devices

With the continuing increase in vehicular traffic, especially in the big cities, and the continuing explosion in road and highway building to accommodate an increasingly mobile America, the use of effective warning devices on ambulances became imperative to assure speedy, safe passage on their life-saving missions, and to protect the lives of both patients and crew.

By the end of the decade, no emergency-type ambulance could be considered fully equipped without a modern electric siren. Bells and gongs were no longer enough. By the late 1920s several well-known companies were marketing electric sirens for emergency vehicles, including auto ambulances. They included the Sterling Siren Fire Alarm Co. of Rochester, New York; The Sireno Corp., Inc. of Staten Island, New York; the Federal Electric Company of Chicago, Illinois; and on the West Coast, the B&M Siren Manufacturing Co. of Los Angeles and the C.A.M. Mfg. Co. of San Francisco, California.

Among the most popular of these was Sterling's Model 12. With its trumpet-type projector, this familiar siren remained in production into the 1940s. In most cases, the siren was mounted on the front of the car in front of the radiator—usually on the chassis frame extension or on the headlight tie bar. In other instances the siren was mounted on the car's running board, on either side of the cowl or on a front fender, usually on the left. Some ambulances were equipped with concealed underhood sirens driven off the engine's fan belt.

Well-equipped ambulances of the day were also often equipped with one or two flashing red warning lights. The S&M Lamp Company of Los Angeles was a prominent manufacturer of these, which were sold as S&M Red Safety-Lites. The Dietz Company of Syracuse, New York, was also a prominent supplier of red warning lights. Red flashers were usually mounted on the windshield pillars. A single flashing red light was sometimes mounted on the front bumper or on the headlight tie bar in front of the radiator.

A swivel-type spotlight, which could be manually aimed from inside the car—indispensable for checking street addresses on night calls—was frequently mounted on the front bumper, or on the headlight tie bar in front of the radiator.

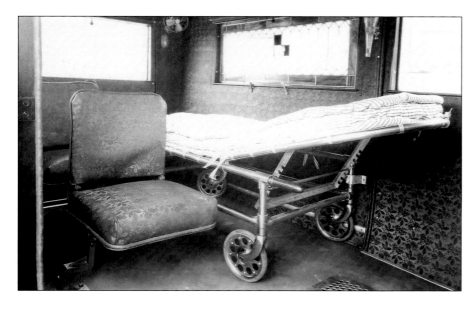

Interior view of Flxible-Buick ambulance of the late 1920s. Note ceiling fan, attendant's seat and cheery flower vase above cot.

Two views of 1926 Dodge Bros. ambulance built for Meriden, Connecticut. Body builder unknown. Note folding attendant's seat in left foregound, second seat attached to partition.

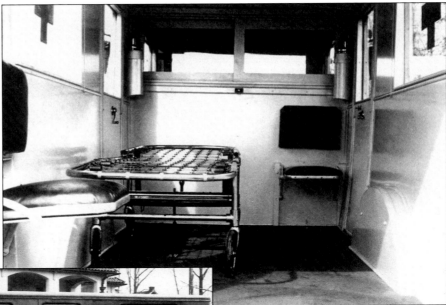

Luxury type 1927 Henney "landau back" limousine ambulance built for Detroit Receiving Hospital. Note padded leather top, carriage lamps on front door pillars.

Well-appointed ambulance of the late 1920s. Knightstown Body Company mounted limousine ambulance body on 1928 Packard chassis. Note siren above bumper, flashing red light on roof.

Meteor Model 215 limousine ambulance, 1924. Meteor and less expensive Mort were on assembled chassis. Note stained glass in rear side windows, tiny bell in front of radiator.

1926 Superior-Cadillac limousine ambulance. Note frosted rear windows with etched ambulance cross. Bus builder Superior Body Company of Lima, Ohio began making hearses, ambulances in 1925.

1926 Cunningham limousine ambulance used by Strong Memorial Hospital, Rochester, New York. Note big drum headlights, "ambulance" signboard on roof.

Cadillac marketed its own hearses and ambulances in the mid-to-late 1920s. Limousine style bodies were built for Cadillac by Meteor. This is the 1928 Cadillac "custom-built" ambulance.

Special Cunningham armored ambulance built for J. T. Hinton & Son of Memphis, Tennessee, in 1927. Rationale for the armor had been lost to time.

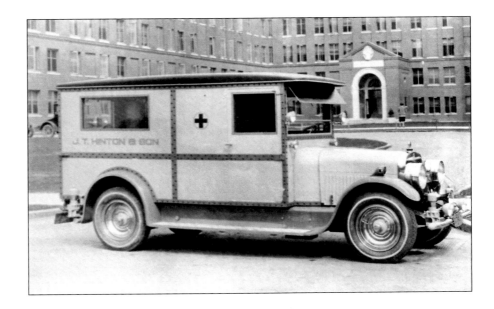

1927 Henney combination hearse/ambulance restored by Bill Alexander of Herndon, Virginia. John W. Henney Company of Freeport, Illinois built ambulances, funeral cars on its own assembled chassis.

A. J. Miller open-front town car ambulance on 1929 Packard Eight chassis. Note vertical v-type windshield and wicker infant basket visible through rear side door.

Wayne Weber displayed this 1930 Oakland sedan-type ambulance at a 1995 PCS Meet. Right-hand doorpost and right front seat could be removed to accommodate ambulance cot.

Brantford Coach & Body Company of Brantford, Ontario built Henney hearse and ambulance bodies for the Canadian market. This nicely preserved 1939 Brantford/Henney-Packard ambulance served Kitchener-Waterloo General Hospital.

Depression, and the Age of Automotive Style 1930 - 1939

For the North American auto industry it was the **best** of times and the **worst** of times. The 1930s was a decade of crushing economic depression, massive unemployment, terrible drought and hard times. But the "dirty thirties" was also the Golden Age of the Automobile—the gilded era of the classic car.

No single decade in the history of the automobile was marked by such a dramatic transformation in vehicle styling and appearance. The typical passenger car (and ambulance) of 1930 had a stodgy rectangular profile with flat, vertical windshield and exposed radiator. The spare tire was lashed to the cowl (premium models sported two side-mounted spares). The "trunk" was precisely that—a steamer style trunk that was strapped to an external carrier at the rear of the car.

In stark contrast, the typical passenger car of 1939 was dramatically lower and streamlined, with shapely pontoon fenders, a long, tapered hood and prow, a V-type windshield and an integrated trunk. The radiator had disappeared behind a chrome-trimmed grille that imparted an unmistakable vehicle identity. One can only wonder what other advances **might** have been made had the auto industry **not** been hobbled by the Great Depression.

The most significant advances of the 1930s included the advent of streamlined, aerodynamic styling and the replacement of wood-framed bodies by far stronger and safer all-steel welded bodies. Composite roofs gave way to all-steel "turret" tops. During the 1930s, streamlining reshaped the world around us—not just passenger cars and trucks. Everything from household appliances and furniture to railway locomotives and skyscrapers took on an ultra-modern, streamlined art deco look.

No doubt influenced by the recently organized "art and color" styling studios set up by the major auto companies, aerodynamic styling (streamlining) began to influence automotive design in a big way starting in 1933. First came sweeping, deep-skirted fenders and smartly raked radiators. Ventilator doors replaced hood louvers. Side-mounted spare tires were buried deeper in the curvaceous front fenders and enclosed under stylish metal covers. Aircraft-type "V" windshields were swept back at ever more daring angles, and headlights were bullet- or acorn-shaped—or hidden altogether.

The dazzling design and engineering advances now introduced on an annual basis by the major automakers were, of course, immediately embraced by the professional car industry. In 1933, the A. J. Miller Company applied pleasing "beavertail" styling to the rear of its limousine style professional car bodies.

Instead of "tucking under," the body sheet metal below the rear doorsill curved outward, neatly filling the gap that formerly existed between the body and the rear bumper.

While streamlining and all-steel bodies were the most important advances made by the auto industry during the 1930s, the introduction of the factory-built, long-wheelbase *"commercial chassis"* was the most significant advance in professional car construction in this milestone decade.

Until the mid-1930s, the hearse and ambulance manufacturer had to literally cut the base passenger car chassis in two, then fabricate and insert a new center section to increase the wheelbase to the required length for mounting a hearse or ambulance body. While initially strong enough to do the job, these cut-and-spliced chassis extensions inevitably loosened up, developing squeaks and rattles no mechanic could ever expunge. As the passenger cars used as the basis for funeral cars and ambulances became quieter and more sophisticated, something better was clearly needed.

General Motors and Packard were the first to offer *factory-built* bare commercial-type chassis designed and engineered exclusively for the mounting of hearse and ambulance bodies. Introduced in 1934-1935, these new commercial chassis featured a one-piece ladder-type, "X"-braced frame. The auto manufacturer also equipped these chassis with a factory-lengthened propeller shaft and heavy-duty brake and suspension components.

The factory-built commercial chassis consisted of the frame and power train (engine, transmission, propeller shaft, differential and rear axle); front-end sheet metal forward of the cowl including hood, fenders, grille, instrument panel and steering wheel. A temporary seat—little more than a wooden milk crate—was provided so the chassis could be driven on and off the truck or rail car which delivered it from the factory in Detroit to the professional car builder's factory in Ohio, Indiana or Illinois. Rear fenders, windshield and front seat were shipped separately. The ambulance or hearse body, designed and built entirely by the independent professional car builder, was lowered onto this special chassis.

General Motors offered a 160-inch wheelbase Cadillac commercial chassis powered by the division's 346-cubic-inch Flathead V-8 engine. Cadillac also offered the professional car trade a slightly less expensive

Los Angeles Fire Department's Rescue Co. 1 shows off its 1930 Superior-Studebaker rescue ambulance. Where did they stow all that gear?

LaSalle commercial chassis powered by LaSalle's Oldsmobile-derived straight eight. For 1935, the Packard Motor Car Company introduced a 158-inch wheelbase commercial chassis version of its moderately priced new Packard One-Twenty. Packard's Model 120A commercial chassis was powered by a 257-cubic-inch, 110-horsepower straight eight.

For the first time, America's two largest luxury carmakers were working hand in hand with the specialty hearse and ambulance manufacturers. Over the years this would prove a mutually beneficial arrangement. The factory-built commercial chassis would literally constitute the backbone of the American hearse and ambulance industry for the next 49 years!

Almost without exception, ambulances of the 1930s were of the classic limousine body style, with two elongated windows on each side of the car behind the front doors. The rearmost side windows were fitted with ornamental beveled, leaded glass, usually with a cross design at their center to unmistakably identify the vehicle as an ambulance. Later in the decade frosted glass was also used.

Pull-down window blinds afforded privacy for the patient when needed. Toward the end of the decade, the rear compartment windows of some premium model ambulances were equipped with horizontal Venetian-type blinds.

As noted, this was the age of **style** in American automobile design. The most severely formal passenger car body style of the classic era was the stately open-front Town Car. A smartly uniformed chauffeur drove this aristocratic limousine from a leather-trimmed open front compartment while his well-heeled passengers rode in coddled luxury on plush mohair or broadcloth upholstery in the opulently appointed rear compartment. Communication with the driver was via speaking tube.

It didn't take long for America's professional car builders to adopt this most aristocratic of body styles for its most exclusive funeral cars and ambulances. Sayers & Scovill of Cincinnati introduced its first open-front "town car" ambulance for 1930. The stunning S&S Worthington Metropolitan Town Car Ambulance featured leaded rear

The Town Car"

Notice the metropolitan "town car" effect of the aristocratic S&S Worthington. A special cover, quickly and easily adjusted, shelters the driver's compartment in inclement weather.

"The Invalid Car Supreme"—a stately 1930 Sayers & Scovill "Worthington" Metropolitan Town Car Invalid Coach. Canvas roof buttoned into place over chauffeur's compartment.

The essence of style...a 1930 Silver-Knightstown Buick Town Car Invalid Coach built for P. J. Ryan & Sons Funeral Home of Terre Haute, Indiana.

1931 Superior-Studebaker Samaritan Ambulance on President Eight chassis in service with Nutley, New Jersey Police Department.

windows with ruby-Red Cross emblems; exterior mounted carriage lamps, and eye-catching three-tone paint. This model, on S&S's own assembled hearse and ambulance chassis, was produced in very small numbers through 1934. The A. J. Miller Company also built some open-front town car ambulances on Packard and Cadillac chassis. Superior advertised a Pierce-Arrow Town Car Ambulance. The National Casket Company even offered a Henney-built town car limousine ambulance on a Reo Royale chassis.

The typical single-purpose emergency ambulance of this era had a fixed partition between the driver's compartment and the patient compartment in the rear. Sliding glass windowpanes permitted communication with the driver. Medicine cabinets were built into the lower part of the partition, along with separate compartments for sheets, blankets, etc. A cot holder was attached to the left wheel well to securely hold the wheeled ambulance stretcher during transport.

One or two folding seats were provided for medical attendants. Deluxe-type ambulances were equipped with wicker bassinets for transporting babies or infants. This baby basket was transversely mounted on the upper portion of the divider partition. In addition to all of the standard medical equipment,

Luxury type limousine ambulance on a 1931 Cadillac V-8 chassis by the A. J. Miller Company. Note chrome-plated wheel discs, sweep panel on cowl, cadet-type windshield visor.

A true classic—1932 Silver-Knightstown Cadillac V-12 ambulance. Very few professional cars were built on expensive Cadillac V-12 and V-16 chassis.

A nicely restored 1932 A. J. Miller-Nash "Adams Senior" limousine ambulance. Ambulances of this vintage are very rare today.

37

the well-equipped ambulance now carried an Emerson or E&J Resuscitator.

Generally speaking, ambulance service in the U.S. was still provided by three principal providers—hospitals, the municipal boards of health and, most commonly, by local funeral homes. Some fire departments also provided ambulance service and—especially in the northeastern U.S.—volunteer first aid and rescue squads provided emergency ambulance service. Local legion posts, service clubs and ladies' auxiliaries supported these services with donations of funds and equipment, sometimes including the ambulance itself.

It was during this decade that the dual-purpose **Combination Coach** really emerged as a distinct type of professional car. The versatile combination—which would be an industry staple for the next four decades—was designed for use as either a hearse **or** ambulance. The local undertaker could thus use a single vehicle for two distinctly different purposes.

The typical combination hearse/ambulance was invariably of the limousine body style. When it was to be used as an ambulance, window drapes were removed, "Ambulance" grilles were inserted in the rear quarter windows and the casket rack with rollers was removed, leaving a flat linoleum or mohair-covered floor. An ambulance cot

1931 Flxible-Buick limousine ambulance. Note two-tone paint job, leaded glass rear windows and big siren mounted on chassis frame extension.

Rear view of Flxible-Buick ambulance of the early 1930s. Note rescue tools carried in special rear door compartment.

was held in place by a locking device that attached to the left wheel housing. An "Ambulance" nameplate replaced the "Funeral Coach" nameplate in the windshield to complete the transformation. A flashing red light or mechanical siren was mounted above the front bumper, although some combinations were equipped with underhood sirens. Although most combination coaches of this period were painted standard funeral black, some were painted in neutral colors such as gray or silver-blue.

As flexible as the two-cars-in-one combination was, it must have been decidedly discomforting for a patient to wake up on the way to the hospital to realize that they were traveling in something that was obviously more hearse than ambulance!

By the late 1930s, the American professional car industry had truly come of age. The vast majority of the ambulances built in the United States were the products of a dozen nationally recognized hearse manufacturers. The major players included:

- Sayers & Scovill Company—Cincinnati, Ohio
- The Superior Coach Corporation—Lima, Ohio
- The Meteor Motor Car Company—Piqua, Ohio
- The A. J. Miller Company—Bellefontaine, Ohio
- The Flxible Company—Loudonville, Ohio
- James Cunningham, Son & Company—Rochester, New York
- The Henney Motor Company—Freeport, Illinois
- The Eureka Company—Rock Falls, Illinois
- Silver-Knightstown Body Company—Knightstown, Indiana
- Knightstown Funeral Car Company—Knightstown, Indiana
- The Shop of Siebert Associates—Toledo, Ohio

In addition to these well-known nameplates, dozens of other smaller firms such as the Crown Coach Corporation of Los Angeles, also built ambulances on various chassis. Many of these were regional, rather than national, builders and distributors.

Remarkably, only one of the industry's established players succumbed to the ravages of the Great Depression. James Cunningham, Son & Company ceased all vehicle production—including hearses and ambulances—at the end of 1936, just two

What a find! This remarkably complete, original 1933 Studebaker ambulance is towed out of a barn in Indiana after decades of storage.

years shy of what would have been its centennial. Cunningham had long been known for its expensive, premium grade hearses and ambulances. This company was but one of the many casualties of the Depression, which killed off many independent auto companies and custom body builders with chilling impartiality. Such well-known names as Pierce-Arrow, Auburn, Franklin, Cord, Duesenberg and Marmon died along with most of the custom body business.

At the opposite end of the price spectrum from Cunningham was the Shop of Siebert Associates, which **entered** the professional car industry at the depths of the Depression, in 1933. But Siebert, of Toledo, Ohio, specialized in low-budget hearses, ambulances, combinations and limousines built on stretched Ford V-8 chassis. Smaller funeral parlors and undertakers who could not afford a new Cadillac, Packard or Buick hearse or ambulance **could** afford a shiny new Ford.

One of the milestone corporate developments during the 1930s was the deal signed in 1937 under which the Henney Motor Company shrewdly negotiated exclusive rights to the Packard commercial chassis. From that point forward, Henney—and **only** Henney—was allowed to mount hearse and ambulance bodies on the highly respected Packard commercial chassis. Considered a major coup for John W. Henney at the time, this exclusive arrangement would ultimately lead to the company's downfall less than two decades later.

Patient comfort was increasingly important to ambulance operators. Sayers & Scovill offered air conditioning in its Parkway ambulances in 1937. The following year Henney introduced what it called the industry's first mechanically-refrigerated air conditioning system for its Packard ambulances. Supplied to Henney by Trane, the one-ton capacity air conditioning unit was mounted at the rear of the car. Power was supplied by a 110-volt generator. Cool air was delivered to the patient compartment through grilles in the rear wheel wells.

By 1939, the first modern **high-head-room** ambulances were being built by Sayers & Scovill and Knightstown. These heavy-duty rescue-type ambulances could transport as many as four patients with ample headroom for the physician or attendants to administer first aid en route to the hospital.

After the devastating Depression, a measure of cautious prosperity had returned to the country. But war clouds were gathering on the horizon.

Recently restored 1933 McLaughlin-Buick combination hearse/ambulance built by Mitchell Hearse Company of Ingersoll, Ontario, Canada.

Canadian-built 1933 McLaughlin-Buick combination hearse/ambulance built by Mitchell Hearse Company. Owned and restored by John Kellam of Pickering, Ontario, Canada.

Interior of John Kellam's 1933 McLaughlin-Buick combination. Note two forward-facing attendant's seats, nicely finished wooden linen cabinet.

<u>Warning Devices</u>

With the continuing tremendous increase in vehicular traffic, better roads and higher vehicle speeds, effective audio and visual warning devices had become essential for all types of emergency vehicles. No modern ambulance could be considered complete without a penetrating mechanical siren, a flashing red light mounted on the front fender or bumper, or a pair of flashing red cowl lights by Dietz or S&M.

In the early 1930s, the Buckeye Iron & Brass Works of Dayton, Ohio, introduced an oscillating warning light called the Moto-Ray. Driven by a small electric motor, the Moto-Ray's beam of red light swept from side to side... "Sweeping Danger Out Of The Way!" In 1934, the Mars Light Company of Oak Park, Illinois, introduced a new type of emergency warning light, which it advertised as "The Light From Mars." This light oscillated from side-to-side while the reflector inside moved up and down, casting a powerful "figure eight" beam of red light ahead and to both sides of the vehicle.

Other articulated "wig-wag" warning lights were also introduced in the mid-1930s. One of the most distinctive of these was the art deco Akr-O-Lite made by Akron Brass. This stylish new light featured a bomb-shaped lower casing complete with airship-style fins. The motor-driven red light atop this distinctive warning device oscillated from side to side.

Another effective vehicular warning signal was the Buckeye's famed Roto-Ray. Available in two sizes, the Roto-Ray had three separate motor-driven red lights that whirled like a pinwheel. The effect was a spinning circle of red that could be seen for blocks. The senior Buckeye Roto-Ray was widely used on motor fire apparatus, but the smaller Junior Roto-Rays were often fitted to better grade ambulances.

In the latter part of the decade, a whole new generation of streamlined, chrome-plated sirens—some with an oscillating red light built into the front—made their appearance. The most popular of these were the Sterling 20 and 30 Sirenlite; Federal's Model WL, Model "Z" with small red "bulls eye"; the big C5, and C6 Traffik-King, Model 77; and B&M's Big Chief Siro-Drift. By the end of the decade, these high-styled, bullet-shaped sirens were usually mounted on the car's roof above the "V"-type windshield, or on the left front fender.

The H.O.R. Company of Staten Island, New York, marketed a popular underhood siren that was driven off the vehicle's fan belt.

Ambulances were most commonly painted white or ivory, often with contrasting fenders, belt and window moldings. Red was popular, too. Many privately operated ambulances were still painted in distinctive hues to match the livery of the funeral homes or the institutions that operated them.

Attractive two-toned 1935 Flxible-Buick Premier limousine ambulance. This photograph taken on lawn of the Flxible Company plant, Loudonville, Ohio.

Henney-Packard Model 1205 "Hospital Ambulance" on 1935 Super Eight chassis. Note wire wheels, illuminated "ambulance" light in front of grille.

At left. 1935 Chrysler Airstream ambulance, California. Body appears to be by Crown Carriage & Body, Los Angeles, California.

Below. Henney Motor Company marketed "Henney Arrowline" hearses, ambulances on Pierce-Arrow chassis from 1934 to 1936. Hoffmeister Mortuary of St. Louis, Missouri operated 1936 Henney Arrowline Model 1264 ambulance powered by Pierce-Arrow Straight Eight.

Meteor Motor Car Company built this awesome one-off ambulance on a 1937 Cadillac V-16 chassis for the Detroit Fire Department. Huge limousine body was transferred to a new Cadillac V-8 chassis in 1951.

1937 Packard One-Twenty limousine ambulance built by Knightstown Body Company. Note carriage lamps mounted on front door pillar, big coaster siren between grille and right front fender.

Ivory-colored 1937 Henney-Packard Model 874 ambulance on 158-inch wheelbase Packard One-Twenty "CA" commercial chassis.

Introduced in 1934, the LaSalle commercial chassis was very popular with hearse and ambulance builders through 1940. This is a 1937 A. J. Miller-LaSalle limousine ambulance. Note ornamental leaded rear side windows.

Fleet of Flxible ambulances operated by Schaefer's Ambulance Service, Los Angeles. Lineup includes three 1938 Flxible-LaSalles and one 1937 Flxible-Buick. The '38s sport stylish new "tunnel" roof lights.

This 1938 A. J. Miller-Dodge ambulance sports up-to-date warning devices. Federal "WL" siren on left front fender, Mars light on roof.

1939 Flxible-LaSalle limousine ambulance built for the Branchville Rescue Squad, Prince Georges County, Maryland. Note big roof-mounted Federal siren.

Sayers & Scovill Company custom-built this special high-headroom ambulance on a 1939 Cadillac V-8 chassis for Cincinnati General Hospital.

Classic Silver-Knightstown limousine ambulance on a 1939 Lincoln "K" series chassis for Misericordia Hospital. Note front-mounted fire apparatus bell and projector-type siren.

46

Ambulance bodies were mounted on every conceivable chassis. This is a Knightstown ambulance on a shark-nosed 1939 Graham Supercharged chassis.

Beautifully restored 1939 Henney-Packard Model 894 ambulance owned by Wayne Kempfert, Plymouth, Minnesota. Photograph taken by the author at the Packard Centennial Celebration in Warren, Ohio in July 1999.

Beautifully restored 1940 Flxible-Buick ambulance owned by Paul Vickery of Summit, New Jersey. Car is finished in dark green.

Flxible introduced all-new Buick professional cars for 1949. This is a 1949 Flxible-Buick Premier ambulance on Roadmaster chassis with a Dynaflow automatic transmission.

War and Rebirth
1940 - 1949

In a much different way, the 1940s would prove an even more eventful decade than the one that preceded it. As the decade began, war was already raging in Europe. It would be only a matter of time before America was drawn into the conflict.

By 1940, the nation had largely recovered from the ravages of the Great Depression and American industry—already profiting from huge orders from the British Empire for armaments and supplies to fight the war raging overseas—had entered a new era of relative prosperity. So, too, had U.S. automobile and professional car manufacturers. Business was good....

By 1940, running boards had all but vanished from passenger cars, as had the side-mounted spare tire. Wide new bodies, sweeping fastback rooflines and integral front fenders were the new style of the day. Grilles were larger and increasingly chrome-accented. Cars had developed strong visual identities: any ten-year-old boy could tell a Ford from a Buick from a Packard or DeSoto.

Prior to the war U.S. ambulance production was, in the main, dominated by the dozen or so companies listed in the previous chapter. With exclusive rights to the Packard commercial chassis, the Henney Motor Company had emerged as the industry's leading player. The Henney plant in Freeport, Illinois, built a record 1,200 Packard hearses, ambulances, combinations, flower and service cars during the booming 1940 model year.

Cadillac's moderately priced companion car, the LaSalle, was discontinued at the end of the 1940 model year—and with it the extremely popular LaSalle Series 50 commercial chassis. For 1941 Cadillac replaced the LaSalle with a new 163-inch Series 62 commercial chassis, which was sold along with the more expensive Series 75. The 1941 Cadillacs—including professional cars built on the new commercial chassis—were arguably some of the best-looking cars ever made. Cadillac's handsome new front-end ensemble with its rectangular "eggcrate" grille seemed especially well-suited to ambulance and funeral car body architecture.

Rival Packard continued to annually refine its tall, distinctive radiator. As successful as the Packard continued to be, the 1941 Cadillac was a much more modern looking car—until the arrival of the stunning new Packard Clipper in mid-1941. But there was to be no Clipper commercial chassis.

The versatile Combination Funeral Coach/Ambulance continued to gain in popularity. The A. J. Miller Company's Duplex Combination featured "Tu-Level" floor, with attendant seats which neatly folded out of sight into the car's floor when the coach was used as a hearse. Flip-over floor panels had mohair upholstery and casket rollers on one side, and hard-wearing linoleum on the other.

Despite the escalating war in Europe, the vigorous momentum generated by 1940 and 1941 vehicle sales rolled unabated on into the 1942 model year. Cadillac and Packard made only modest changes to their commercial chassis, but The Flxible Company had a totally restyled new Buick on which to base its all-new hearse and ambulance bodies. With its wide, low-set grille and long pontoon fenders which extended into the front doors and high, bullnosed hood, the new Buick made for an imposing professional car.

Everything changed after December 7, 1941. With the Japanese attack on Pearl Harbor, America was thrust into the cauldron of the Second World War. Almost overnight, American industry shifted to all-out war production. Suddenly there were material shortages and strict rationing. The last new civilian automobiles and professional cars "for the duration" rolled off the assembly lines in February 1942.

Ambulance operators and funeral directors would have to "make do" with whatever vehicles they had been able to purchase before the curtain came down. What few civilian-type ambulances were still being built on leftover 1942 commercial chassis were being diverted to the war effort. Very few passenger car-based ambulances were made during the war—virtually all for the armed

forces or various government agencies. Most of these "metropolitan" or municipal-type commercial-chassis ambulances stayed stateside while thousands of special military field ambulances—khaki or olive-drab boxes mounted on military or modified commercial truck chassis of one to two-and-a-half tons—were built by the major automakers and shipped to war fronts overseas.

One of the most interesting ambulances produced during the Second World War was a special "Civilian Defense Ambulance" built by the Henney Motor Company. Constructed on the 160-inch wheelbase 1942 Packard commercial chassis, this vehicle was designed to transport four patients on standard army-type stretchers, along with ample headroom for four attendants. To conserve rationed rubber, the CD ambulance rode on single rear tires.

"Henney engineers have developed an entirely new type of stretcher support which enables women, elderly men or inexperienced helpers to load four stretcher patients into the ambulance all from the outside," the brochure stated.

Instead of the usual limousine style body, Henney's Civilian Defense Ambulance had

1940 Henney-Packard Model 4094 limousine ambulance used by Genessee Hospital, Rochester, New York. Note dual remote control spotlights, Sterling Model 30 Sirenlite on roof.

Stylish 1940 Flxible-Buick limousine ambulance. Note contrasting two-tone paint, streamlined "tunnel" lights on roof and optional rear wheel fender skirts.

War was again raging in Europe. Donated to the government of Finland, this 1940 Superior-Pontiac Guardian ambulance was photographed on a New York pier before being loaded aboard ship.

High-headroom 1941 Cadillac ambulance built by Silver-Knightstown Body Company, Knightstown, Indiana. These big rescue-type ambulances were especially popular with rescue squads in New Jersey.

Factory-fresh 1941 Eureka-Cadillac limousine ambulance photographed at Lawrence Park in Rock Falls, Illinois. Note front-mounted Mars "wig wag" light, roof tunnel lights.

1941 Sayers & Scovill Cadillac ambulance owned by Herold Berthy of Morgantown, West Virginia. Note distinctive S&S trim on front of hood.

Handsome white-painted 1941 Flxible-Buick ambulance operated by Angelus Funeral Home, Los Angeles, California. Note red lens on left side spotlight. Siren was mounted under hood.

a rectangular box-type body grafted onto a standard Packard passenger car front-end rearward of the front doors. This vehicle presaged the Type III modular ambulance by nearly three decades! The vehicle's unique styling featured ambulance cross-shaped side windows, a theme that was repeated on the double rear doors—a throwback to the early days of motor ambulances.

Like the auto companies, the professional car manufacturers also quickly converted to defense production. Sayers & Scovill (renamed Hess & Eisenhardt after sons of two longtime S&S employees purchased the company during the war) produced seven different types of military vehicles, including tank recovery and track-laying trailers. The Henney Motor Company also built a wide range of specialized vehicles for the Army and Navy as well as precision parts for Rolls-Royce aircraft engines—the renowned Packard Merlin. The Eureka Company built field ambulances for the Army on Chevrolet truck chassis, as well as eight-door, 15-passenger "war workers" buses on stretched Chevrolet car chassis and 100-passenger bus trailers for the Chicago Ordnance District.

Superior Coach and Flxible—both major bus manufacturers—built many types of buses and specialized vehicles for the U.S. military. The Shop of Siebert built 15-passenger bus conversions of Ford sedans and also produced parts for the Republic P-47 Thunderbolt fighter plane.

With their supply of chassis cut off, there were inevitably some casualties in the industry. By 1943, both the Knightstown Funeral Car Company and Silver-Knightstown had closed the doors of their Knightstown, Indiana, factories.

By 1944, America was clearly winning the war and auto and professional car manufacturers started to plan for the resumption of peacetime vehicle production. While war contracts were still being fulfilled, the first postwar vehicles were beginning to take shape on the drawing boards. When victory was declared in 1945, the auto companies immediately began to retool their plants to meet unprecedented demand for new motor vehicles of all types—including funeral cars and ambulances.

Cadillac resumed production of its 163-inch Series 75 commercial chassis toward

1941 Superior-Cadillac "Metropolitan-type" hospital ambulance built for U.S. Army Medical Service. Note roof-mounted clearance lights, blanked-out center side windows.

the end of 1945, just in time for the 1946 model year. Superior, A. J. Miller, Hess & Eisenhardt, Meteor and Eureka wasted no time in introducing their 1946-model hearses and ambulances. The Flxible Company also resumed professional car production—now exclusively on elongated Buick chassis. At last, funeral directors and ambulance operators who had pampered their prewar equipment through the war years could finally order new replacement vehicles.

Industry leader Henney, however, found itself in an embarrassing situation. Unlike its competitors, Packard did not resume commercial chassis production immediately after the war. Instead of placing dated pre-war chassis back into production, Packard opted to design a completely new commercial chassis and stylish new funeral coach, ambulance, flower and service car bodies for 1948.

Consequently, except for one Clipper-based prototype, the Henney Motor Company built **no** 1946 or 1947-model funeral coaches or ambulances. Instead, the Henney production line at Freeport was kept busy turning out taxi and eight-passenger limousine bodies for Packard.

The first postwar American passenger cars—and professional vehicles—were little more than warmed-over versions of 1942 models. True, there were engineering re-

More than a few former hearses were later converted into ambulances. This 1941 Henney-Packard ambulance was photographed at the 1994 PCS International Meet in Pittsburgh, Pennsylvania.

Rare, one-off ambulance conversion of a 1941 Lincoln Continental V-12 limousine, builder unknown. This spectacular ambulance is part of the Fred Hunter Collection, Fort Lauderdale, Florida.

finements and cosmetic changes to grilles, emblems and instrument panels, but several years would pass before the industry's first all-new postwar models made their splashy debuts.

As welcomed as it was, postwar vehicle production did not resume smoothly. There were lengthy strikes and serious material shortages—especially of steel, chrome and tires. More than a few 1946-model cars were shipped with wooden plank bumpers and wartime-style painted trim. In the meantime, ambulance operators and funeral directors were clamoring for new equipment to replace their worn-out prewar vehicles. It was a seller's market. Anything new on wheels commanded a premium price. More often than not, a buyer's name went on a long waiting list.

Henney's all-new 1948 models were introduced with appropriate fanfare in mid-1947. The 1948 Henney-Packard funeral coaches, ambulances, combinations and flower and service cars featured the same controversial "bathtub" styling as the rest of the Packard Motor Car company's Twenty-Second Series

Relatively few Cadillac commercial chassis were delivered in the war-shortened 1942 model year. This big buff-colored 1942 Flxible-Cadillac ambulance was built for the Connecticut State Police.

Landau body style appeared in the late 1930s. This is a 1942 Flxible-Buick Model B72G landau ambulance. Note chrome-plated landau irons spanning closed upper rear quarter panel, Federal 78 Traffic-King siren on roof.

Presaging modern modular ambulances, Henney Motor Company introduced a special "civil defense ambulance" with cube-type body in 1942. This one was donated to the Chicago Fire Department by American Legion Post #206.

Shop of Siebert specialized in low-budget hearse and ambulance conversions of Fords and Mercurys. Rochester, New York Department of Public Safety operated this 1942 Siebert-Ford municipal ambulance.

1946 Siebert-Ford municipal-type ambulance conversion of a 1946 Ford half-ton panel truck. Wheelbase was stretched to 150 inches.

passenger cars. The 1948 Henney-Packard was built on an all-new 160-inch wheelbase Packard commercial chassis powered by a 215-hosepower straight-eight engine.

Introduced just before the war on 1940 Oldsmobiles, then on 1941 Cadillacs and Buicks, GM's Hydra-Matic automatic transmission found much favor with professional car buyers.

Most of the ambulances built in the booming postwar era were of the classic limousine body style—although a few style-conscious operators preferred the more formal landau. White and red remained the most popular color choices for ambulances, although any monotone or two-tone combination desired by the purchaser could be ordered. Because of their propensity to fade or turn yellow, white or ivory paint jobs weren't guaranteed by professional car builders.

By 1948, the professional car industry had shifted into overdrive. Every car that rolled off the assembly line was eagerly snapped up by a car-hungry profession. To meet this unprecedented demand, and to cope with the problem of sharply increased postwar vehicle prices, a new genre of professional car appeared in 1947-1948. It was the long-wheelbase "economy" model professional car.

Many funeral directors—most of whom still provided ambulance service to their communities—simply could no longer afford to buy a new Cadillac, Packard or Buick ambulance, hearse or combination. To address this need, several new professional car manufacturers arrived on the scene. These companies specialized in hearse, ambulance and combination coach conversions of the light-duty sedan delivery vehicles now being marketed in sizeable numbers by Pontiac and Chevrolet.

The Sedan Delivery was essentially a two-door station wagon body shell without side windows. All one had to do to convert one of these stylish, yet practical vehicles into a funeral coach or ambulance was to cut it in two and insert a new center section or elongated side door. There was no need to raise the roof or windshield, and the Chevrolet or Pontiac Sedan Delivery even came with a factory-engineered one-piece rear door.

A new *second-tier* professional car industry suddenly sprang up. The principal players included the National Body Mfg. Company of Knightstown, Indiana—the lineal successor to Silver-Knightstown—and a cluster of conversion builders located in and around Memphis, Tennessee—the Guy Barnette Company; Weller Brothers, and the aptly-named Economy Coach Company. The Shop of Siebert Associates of Toledo, Ohio, also continued to do budget-priced hearse and ambulance conversions based on Ford and Mercury passenger cars.

The Cadillac Motor Division of General Motors introduced its first all-new postwar passenger car styling for 1948. The dramatically new 1948 Cadillacs featured fade-away front fenders which flowed into the front doors, a large, curved windshield and a styling feature which would become a Cadillac trademark for the next decade—tailfins! The Cadillac commercial chassis and the division's long-wheelbase Fleetwood Seventy-Five nine-passenger sedan and limousine, however, retained their angular prewar architecture.

The all new 1949 Series 86 commercial chassis not only got Cadillac's fresh new styling with distinctive "fishtail" fins, it was powered by Cadillac's new 331-cubic-inch, high-compression V-8 engine. Cadillac continued to restrict sales of its commercial chassis to five "captive" customers—Superior Coach Corporation, Meteor Motor Car Company, the A. J. Miller Company, Hess & Eisenhardt (S&S) and The Eureka Company. All of these companies designed sleek new professional car bodies for the dramatically lower 1949 commercial chassis.

The Flxible Company also introduced dramatic new styling for the hearses and ambulances on the all-new 1949 Buick Special and Roadmaster chassis, which Flxible cut-and-stretched at its busy plant in Loudonville, Ohio.

In styling and functionality, the 1949 professional cars were indeed a far cry from those of 1940. Such progress, however, would pale in comparison with that of the decade that was about to begin.

Warning Devices

The well-dressed professional ambulance of the 1940s sported a big roof-mounted coaster siren and two alternately flashing red warning lights. On deluxe-type ambulances, these lights were housed in streamlined "tunnels" faired into the leading edge of the roof. Sometimes the siren or a red flashing light was mounted on either—or both—front fenders.

In many communities, sirens were silenced—literally—during the war, when their use was restricted to civil defense air raid warnings. Horns, bells or exhaust whistles were used instead to clear the way. The "wig-wag" light—typified by the oscillating Propello-Ray or Mars light—was also widely used on emergency ambulances.

The most popular ambulance sirens of the 1940s were Federal's C-Series units, the Sterling Sirenlite, the B&M Super Chief and C.A.M. Late in the decade, however, Federal introduced two revolutionary new warning devices which would find widespread use on all types of emergency vehicles for the next two decades.

Federal announced its powerful new "Q" Series mechanical siren in 1948. With its massive rotor, distinctive chrome front with integral "*F*" emblem and bullet-shaped rear cone, the Federal "Q" became one of the most successful warning devices in emergency signal history. The mighty "Q" is still manufactured today, half a century later!

At almost the same time, Federal also introduced a pioneering new type of warning signal light. The company's breakthrough Model 17 "Beacon Ray" had two large red lamps, which revolved 360 degrees under a red plastic dome: the "bubble gum" light had arrived!

Los Angeles county fire department pioneered modern EMS service. The "Father" of EMS and JEMS founder James O. Page is the proud owner of this beautifully restored 1947 Ford panel rescue ambulance.

Milwaukee Fire Department operated this 1947 S&S Cadillac Kensington ambulance for many years. Founded in 1876, Sayers & Scovill was renamed Hess & Eisenhardt Company in the early 1940s, but retained respected S&S name.

Rear view of very original 1947 Miller-Cadillac ambulance still owned by Western Springs (Illinois) Fire Department. This sleekly styled ambulance was photographed at the 1998 PCS International Meet.

Chrysler, DeSoto and Dodge eight-passenger sedans were converted into side-loading sedan ambulances by several conversion companies following the war. This 1947 Chrysler served Edgemont (New Jersey) Life Squad.

John J. C. Little of Ingersoll, Ontario did many sedan ambulance conversions for Canadian funeral directors. This white-painted 1947 Packard Clipper sedan ambulance was built for Holmes Ambulance Service of Dresden, Ontario, Canada.

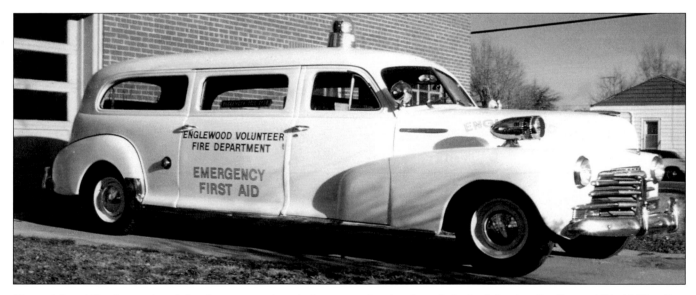

Chevrolet and Pontiac sedan deliveries spawned a whole new professional car industry following the Second World War. Guy Barnette Company of Memphis, Tennessee was one of the major players. This 1948 Barnette-Chevrolet ambulance served the Englewood (Colorado) Fire Department.

Shop of Siebert built low-budget ambulance conversions of Ford and Mercury sedans. This nicely preserved 1948 Siebert-Ford Tu-Way owned by Gene and Steve Lichtman was photographed at the 1989 PCS International Meet in Gaithersburg, Maryland.

Hess & Eisenhardt Company built this 1948 S&S Cadillac deluxe Kensington ambulance with special raised roof. High-headroom ambulances were becoming increasingly popular with rescue squads.

Flxible built many of these big Buick ambulances from 1946 through 1948 to meet pent-up demand for new vehicles to replace pre-war equipment. Note tunnel roof lights, Federal siren and bumper-mounted fog lamps.

Opposite page bottom. Restored 1948 Meteor-Cadillac ambulance owned by Bob Smith, Newcomerstown, Ohio. Distinctive front door with coach lamp was Meteor trademark from 1940 to 1953. Note unique Federal 240-degree roof light.

Flxible custom-built special bus-type ambulance for New York City Fire Department. Based on Flxible Clipper intercity coach, this Fire Department New York disaster ambulance had four beds with space for eight patients. When delivered in 1949, it was described as the largest, most complete ambulance ever built.

Cadillac introduced all-new commercial chassis for 1949. This is a catalog illustration of the handsomely restyled 1949 Superior-Cadillac ambulance.

Henney introduced all new Packard hearses and ambulances for 1948. Twenty-Second and Twenty-Third series Henney-Packards were built from 1948 through 1950. Mark Wilson of Ray Township, Michigan restored this big '48.

Terry Smith of Columbia, Indiana brought this 1949 Miller-Cadillac Duplex combination hearse/ambulance to the 1995 Professional Car Society National Meet. Note red lenses in parking lights, removable "ambulance" grilles in rear side windows.

Catalog illustration of the 1949 Meteor-Cadillac ambulance. Chrome trim below daring "fishtail" fins indicates that chassis may be a '48.

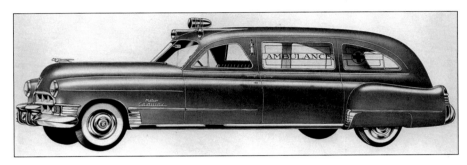

1949 Henney-Packard Model 14994 Ambulance on display at funeral service trade show. By mid year, Twenty-Third series bodies got protective body-side trim, which was utilized through 1950.

Economy Coach Company of Memphis, Tennessee did many ambulance and hearse conversions of Chrysler products. Photographed at a fire apparatus muster in Rochester, Michigan, this 1949 Economy-Dodge ambulance once served Marlette, Michigan.

More hearse than ambulance, this 1950 S&S Cadillac combination has rear window drapes. Parking lamps have been replaced with flashing red lights for ambulance service.

1959 Barnett-Cadillac combination ambulance/funeral coach. Renamed "Barnett" in 1957, this company would be gone within a year.

The Fabulous Fifties
1950 - 1959

If the 1930s was the Golden Age of the Classic Car, then the 1950s was the **Gilded Age** of the American professional car. The truly memorable ambulances and funeral cars of the 1950s reflected the flamboyantly styled, finned, chrome-bedecked, bigger-is-better cars of this colorful era, while at the same time steadily advancing their life-saving efficiency and capabilities.

America went to war again in 1950—this time in far-off Korea. While there were again some restrictions, the Korean War did not affect American industry, nor the civilian populace, to anywhere near the same degree World War II did.

For 1950, Cadillac's Series 86 commercial chassis got fresh, new styling for the second consecutive year. This same basic styling, with minor cosmetic changes, would continue through four model years, from 1950 through 1953. Cadillac's 1950 styling featured a one-piece curved windshield and a massive chrome grille—the beginning of what became known as Cadillac's "million-dollar grin."

The Henney Motor Company's Packard hearses and ambulances entered their third—and final—year with the same controversial "bathtub" styling introduced for 1948. While Henney-Packard sales were still respectable, archrival Cadillac had shifted into high gear and passed its principal competitor—this time for good. Cadillac-based ambulances and funeral cars were now being built by no fewer than five coachbuilders compared to just **one** for Packard: John Henney's "coup" of 1937 had come to haunt the company.

The Chevrolet and Pontiac sedan delivery remained the cornerstone of the thriving economy coach industry. Joining National, Barnette, Economy and Weller Brothers at the low-priced end of the market was yet another new company—the Acme Motor Company of Sterling, Illinois. This local body shop operation began turning out Pontiac sedan delivery hearse and ambulance conversions in 1951. The substantial market for lower-priced professional cars had finally attracted the attention of some of the industry's major players, a few of which—Eureka and Meteor—were now offering long-wheelbase Pontiac hearses, ambulances and combinations of their own, in addition to their top-line Cadillacs.

The big news in the professional car industry for 1951 was the introduction of a totally redesigned line of Henney-Packards. The new Packard commercial chassis was cloaked in attractive new ambulance, funeral coach and combination coach bodies styled by famed industrial designer Richard Arbib. Packard's handsome "new look" featured a wide, low-set grille—a thoroughly up-to-date rendition of the "cusped" radiator, which had unmistakably identified Packards since 1904.

The Arbib look featured softly rounded bodies and, on some models, wraparound rear quarter windows. Alas, this was to be

Henney's last hurrah. Despite the attractive new styling, Henney-Packard sales continued to slide to a fraction of their previous levels.

Barnette and National continued to dominate the conversion coach market. The Economy Coach Company had expanded its product offerings to include more expensive Chrysler hearses and ambulances in addition to its bread-and-butter Chevrolets and Pontiacs. The Shop of Siebert Associates was also doing very well in this segment of the market with both standard and extended-wheelbase Ford and Mercury professional car conversions. Not tied to any particular make, Weller Brothers would design and build an ambulance or funeral car body for virtually any chassis provided by the purchaser.

With increasing urban traffic congestion and continued expansion of the interstate highway system, high-headroom rescue-type ambulances were becoming increasingly popular—especially with fire departments, rescue and first aid squads. While utilizing the same basic limousine body as standard headroom units, these heavy-duty rescue-type ambulances had raised roof panels to permit the vehicle to transport as many as four patients and two or three medical attendants.

Prominent window signs or lettering on the flanks of the most up-to-date ambulances

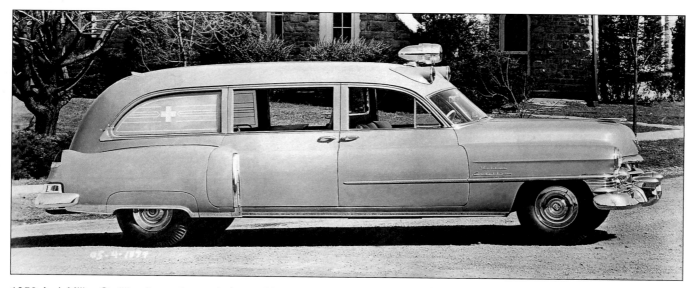

1950 A. J. Miller Cadillac limousine ambulance. Note frosted rear side windows, tunnel lights, big Federal C-series Doubletone siren on roof.

Factory-fresh fleet of five 1950 Flxible-Buick Roadmaster Premier ambulances lined up for delivery to Eastern Ambulance Service of Syracuse, New York.

boasted... **"Radio-Equipped"** or **"Oxygen-Equipped"**—or both.

There were two notable developments in the industry in 1952. The Henney Motor Company introduced the industry's first "compact" professional car and, to the surprise of many, The Flxible Company abandoned the hearse and ambulance business to concentrate on accelerated production of its staple product, intercity buses.

Despite steadily shrinking sales of its long-wheelbase ambulances, hearses, flower cars and combinations, Henney, in a bid for resurgence, came out with the industry's first true **compact** ambulances and funeral cars. Available as an ambulance, funeral car or combination, the new **"Henney Junior"** was a standard-wheelbase Packard Clipper with a raised roof. For the first time, the same high headroom found in a full-sized, long-wheelbase Packard or Cadillac ambulance was now available on a considerably less expensive standard passenger car wheelbase. While the concept was sound, the Henney Junior was not a profitable proposition for its builder. Advertised at an introductory price of $3,333, Henney lost money on every Junior it built. Prices steadily rose to the point where they were within range of the cost of a full-sized Henney-Packard.

The Flxible Company had been one of the industry's best-known players ever since this bus builder entered the hearse and ambulance field in 1925. With its Loudon-ville, Ohio, plant overflowing with lucrative contracts for new buses—many for the U.S. military—Flxible ceased professional car production at the end of the 1952 model year to free up factory floor space for increased bus production. There would be **no** 1953 through 1958 Flxible-Buicks.

The Superior Coach Corporation re-entered the increasingly crowded medium-priced field with an entirely new line of Superior-Pontiac ambulances, hearses and combinations for 1953. Standard-wheelbase Pontiac Star Chief chassis were drop-shipped to Superior's new Southern Division plant in Kosiusko, Mississippi, where they were cut, lengthened and fitted with Superior designed and built limousine or landau ambulance or funeral car bodies. Superior had offered moderately priced Pontiac professional cars before, from 1936 through 1948. Superior-Cadillac ambulance and funeral car production remained at the company's "home" plant in Lima, Ohio.

Taking a cue from the latest passenger car fashions emanating from Detroit, Hess & Eisenhardt introduced stylish rear quarter windows on its 1953 ambulances and funeral cars. These triangular-shaped, curved windows gave S&S professional cars—even somber funeral coaches—a more open, airy look.

While the limousine body style was still favored by most ambulance operators, some funeral directors opted for the formal landau. Most of the principal funeral car

Some of the industry's major players—Meteor and Eureka among them—entered the lower-priced ambulance market in the early 1950s. This is a 1950 Meteor-Pontiac.

and ambulance manufacturers now offered deluxe landau versions of their standard production ambulances and combination coaches. With their closed rear quarters spanned by elegant carriage bows and ornamented with chrome ambulance cross emblems, the landau style ambulance made an impressive and luxurious statement for its owner/operator.

No discussion of ambulances of this era would be complete without special reference to the long-wheelbase sedan-type ambulances used by many small town undertakers, primarily in the Midwest, between 1947 and 1954. Two specialty conversion companies—both located in Michigan—turned out hundreds of practical ambulance/Invalid Car conversions of standard Chrysler, DeSoto and Dodge eight-passenger sedans. The F. H. McClintock Co. of Lansing marketed these popular vehicles as "Sedambulances." The other converter was the Isenhoff Auto Rebuilding Company of Grand Rapids.

The front bench seat was cut in half so the passenger side seat could be easily removed. The right side center doorpost was cut so it could simply be unlatched and removed. A full-sized wheeled ambulance cot, stretcher or wheelchair could then be conveniently loaded into the car's cavernous interior.

By day these dual-purpose vehicles served as dignified pallbearers' sedans or carried bereaved families. But between funerals and after hours, the same car could be used as an emergency ambulance, or to transport the ill or invalid. The Sedambulance concept came to the end of the road when Chrysler Corporation stopped making these relatively inexpensive long-wheelbase sedans at the end of the 1954 model year. Cadillac and Packard eight- and nine-passenger sedans

were too expensive for such modifications, although some such conversions were undoubtedly made.

The year 1954 would be an unusually eventful year for the U.S. professional car industry. Cadillac introduced its first all-new exterior styling in four years. The Model 8680S commercial chassis received Cadillac's fresh, new front-end ensemble with wide "eggcrate" grille and integral bumper "bullets." Wrap-around rear windows were *de rigueur* on most funeral coaches and ambulances (limousine as well as landau body styles).

At the state conventions this year, Superior Coach exhibited a prototype hardtop combination funeral coach and ambulance. Designed to resemble the pillarless four-door hardtops which were sweeping the auto industry, the Superior Cadillac Beau Monde had no "B" or "C" pillars. It was, in essence, a huge five-door hardtop. This high-styled professional car would go into limited production for the 1955-1956 model years.

Hess & Eisenhardt introduced its S&S Cadillac Kensington Hightop ambulance with step-type roof and an optional illuminated Plexiglas name panel across the front.

On the corporate side, the Wayne Works industrial conglomerate of Richmond, Indiana, acquired the Meteor Motor Car Company of Piqua, Ohio. Wayne Works' principal products were school buses and Divco delivery trucks.

After 86 years, the Henney Motor Company quietly ceased hearse, ambulance and limousine production at the end of the 1954 model year. There was **no** commercial chassis in Packard's totally new 1955 product line. C. Russell Feldman, who had purchased the company from John W. Henney in 1946,

Conversion builders—National, Economy, Barnette and Weller Bros.—continued to find a good market for lower-priced Chevrolet and Pontiac ambulances. Ed Sasser brought this 1951 National-Pontiac to the 1994 PCS National Meet.

Catalog illustration of 1951 National-Chevrolet Styleline ambulance. White sidewall tires were an extra-cost option.

Between National's sedan delivery "Ambulette" and the long-wheelbase models was the aptly named National Midway. This is a 1951 National-Pontiac Midway ambulance.

In crisp hospital whites, nurse poses with a 1951 Flxible-Buick Premier ambulance. After 27 years Flxible ended professional car production at the end of the 1952 model year.

simply closed the Freeport factory's doors. Several former Henney executives went over to Superior Coach, which took over as the industry's new leader and style-setter.

Cadillac now dominated the industry.

With the demise of Flxible and Henney, there were now only five principal players left in the industry—all of which used the 158-inch wheelbase Cadillac Series 8680S commercial chassis:

- The Superior Coach Corporation—Lima, Ohio
- The Meteor Motor Car Company—Piqua, Ohio
- The A. J. Miller Company—Bellefontaine, Ohio
- The Hess & Eisenhardt Company—Cincinnati, Ohio
- The Eureka Company—Rock Falls, Illinois

Well-equipped ambulances of the 1950s carried two-way radios and oxygen equipment. Kerr Bros.' 1952 Superior-Cadillac proudly advertised both.

Rear view of 1952 Superior-Cadillac ambulance built for Drake-Flowers funeral service. Note clearance lights on rear roof.

1952 Miller-Cadillac limousine combination. Pale blue hearse/ambulance has airline style drapes in rear windows.

There were changes among some of the smaller players, too. Pontiac and Chevrolet had discontinued their sedan delivery vehicles leaving small players like Acme Coach without a base vehicle on which to build. Converting station wagons proved prohibitively expensive, so Acme closed its doors. The former Economy Coach Company changed its name to the Memphis Coach Company, henceforth branding its products as "Memphians." Many of these were now being built on Chrysler Corporation chassis—Plymouth, Dodge, DeSoto and Chrysler—as well as the occasional Ford and Mercury.

Over the previous decade, several automakers—particularly Chrysler—had vigorously promoted their new steel-bodied station wagons as the basis for economically priced ambulance conversions. While these six/nine-passenger vehicles were quite popular as funeral home utility vehicles, they did not pose any real threat to the established

1952 Eureka-Cadillac Chieftain limousine ambulance. Raked "C" pillar was Eureka styling trademark from 1947 through the firm's demise in 1964. Note fat whitewall tires, red flashers built into parking lights.

Economy Coach Company specialized in Chrysler hearse and ambulance conversions. Phil Gravelle of Scotland, Ontario, Canada found this 1952 Economy-Chrysler ambulance in Florida.

Now residing at the Fort Wayne Fire Museum, this well-preserved 1953 Meteor-Cadillac ambulance previously served Wayne Township, Indiana. This would be the last year for Meteor's trademark coach lamps.

Well-known Packard authority George Hamlin's 1953 Henney-Packard Senior ambulance has participated at PCS Meets since the society began in 1976. Note big, red Henney sports "Mid-Atlantic" nameplates on doors.

1953 Henney-Packard Senior combination funeral car/ambulance owned by Robert Gibbs at Perrysburg Packards Meet in Perrysburg, Ohio in 2001.

professional ambulance builders.

Late in 1955, however, a new specialty company went exclusively into the business of converting station wagons into ambulances and funeral cars. The Automotive Conversion Corporation set up shop in Birmingham, Michigan, just outside of Detroit. This company offered complete "Amblewagon" ambulance and funeral service car conversions of 1956 Ford and Mercury station wagons. ACC would become one of the most successful second-tier players in the industry for the next 25 years.

Another new conversion builder arrived on the scene in 1955. Waldo J. Cotner and Robert F. Bevington had constructed their prototype professional car in a converted garage in Blytheville, Arkansas, in November 1954. The newly-formed Comet Coach Company announced a family of moderately priced hearses, ambulances and combinations built on lengthened 1955 Oldsmobile 88 chassis. Comet moved in to fill the gap between low-line Pontiac and Chevrolet and luxury Cadillac professional cars—the niche abandoned by Flxible a few years earlier.

The industry's structure would change yet again before the end of 1956 when ambitiously expanding Wayne Works purchased the A. J. Miller Company. While retaining both the Meteor and A. J. Miller plants, these two professional car companies were merged into a new entity called the **Miller-Meteor Division**. This consolidation reduced the number of major players in the industry to just four. Production of Meteor-Cadillac funeral coaches and ambulances was phased out of the Piqua, Ohio, plant at the end of the 1956 model year.

The all-new 1957 Miller-Meteor Cadillac professional cars would be produced exclusively at the former A. J. Miller plant in Bellefontaine, Ohio.

The 1957 model year was one of major styling advances for the entire industry, the most sweeping since 1949. The foundation for this change was the all-new "X" frame commercial chassis Cadillac introduced for 1957. This new 156-inch wheelbase chassis was slightly shorter than the 8680S chassis it replaced. The new X-frame configuration resulted in a dramatically lower professional car profile.

Superior designed stunning all-new bodies for this chassis. Superior's bold, new Criterion styling featured thin, arched rooflines and huge glass areas which worked extremely well with the 1957 Cadillac's unique "reversed" tailfins and large wheel cutouts. Hess and Eisenhardt also designed eye-catching new S&S bodies for this chassis. With its 1957 models, The Eureka Company finally abandoned wood-framed body construction in favor of all-steel, welded bodies.

The first Miller-Meteor Cadillac funeral coaches, ambulances, flower cars and com-

Above and opposite page bottom. F. H. McClintock of Lansing, Michigan specialized in side-loading ambulance conversions of Chrysler eight-passenger sedans. Len Langlois of Chatham, Ontario brought this 1953 McClintock/DeSoto "Sedambulance" to the 1998 PCS International Meet at Burr Ridge, Illinois.

binations—introduced for the 1957 model year—also featured thin rooflines and large expanses of glass, especially on the M/M Classic Limousine Ambulance or Combination Funeral Coach & Ambulance. The first Miller-Meteor ambulances were offered in three basic configurations—standard, high-headroom and a premium landau version of the high-headroom unit.

With the brief exception of Cadillac in the mid-1920s, the "Big Three" U. S. auto manufacturers left the hearse and ambulance business to specialty body manufacturers like Superior, S&S, etc. But in late 1957, the smallest of the so-called Big Three dabbled its corporate toes in the professional car pond. The Chrysler Corporation had regularly promoted its top-line station wagons to funeral directors and ambulance operators since 1951. In the fall of 1957, the company's Chrysler Division announced the **Chrysler Brierian**—an extended-headroom conversion of the 1958 Chrysler Town & Country

station wagon. The Brierian offered 39 inches of interior headroom—six inches more than the standard Chrysler wagon—"providing ample room for cardiac patients and attendant's comfort." Brierian conversions were done for Chrysler by Richard Brothers of Eaton Rapids, near Lansing, Michigan.

With the introduction of the industry's 1958 models, the era of the **major** annual styling change had truly arrived. The 1958 Cadillacs were dramatically different from the 1957s. The most noticeable change was up front. The entire U.S. auto industry adopted a new four-headlight road illumination system this year. Two small headlights were paired side by side under each front fender peak. All 1958 Cadillacs—including the 156-inch wheelbase commercial chassis—also sported the rocketship tailfins first seen on the 1955 Cadillac Eldorado.

Superior Coach offered three ambulance roof configurations—the standard 43-inch roof used on the company's hearses and

Here's an oxymoron for you. Economy Coach Company built this luxurious 1953 Chrysler Imperial ambulance for the Department of Public Safety in New Brunswick, New Jersey. Note fire extinguisher carried in left front fender.

Many Chevrolet and Pontiac sedan deliveries were converted into ambulances and funeral cars between 1947 and 1954. Len Langlois of Chatham, Ontario is the proud owner of this 1954 Chevrolet sedan delivery ambulance he found in Iowa.

National Ambulette was low-budget conversion of Chevrolet or Pontiac sedan delivery. This very original 1954 National-Chevrolet Ambulette was photographed at a fire apparatus muster in Michigan.

Henney Motor Company pioneered the compact professional car market with the Packard Clipper-based, standard-wheelbase "Henney Junior" offered in ambulance and combination versions from 1952 to 1954. This is one of two 1954 Henney Juniors owned by Mike Reichenbach.

Below. The last Henney-Packards were built in 1954. This 1954 Henney-Packard Senior ambulance was restored by Metropolitan Toronto Ambulance Service. Note ambulance cross emblem just ahead of wraparound rear windows.

popular combination coaches; a 48-inch high headroom model and a 52-inch high-top. Standard models had an all-steel roof. Extended-headroom models sported a huge, one-piece molded fiberglass roof. Hess & Eisenhardt's Kensington High Body ambulance featured attractive aluminum side roof panels.

This would be the final year for the Memphis Coach Company, which shut its doors at the end of the 1958 model run. Originally organized as the Economy Coach Company in the late 1940s, the company changed its name to Memphis Coach during the 1955 model year. The last Memphians were mostly long-wheelbase Pontiac limousine combinations with airline style window drapes.

National and Comet continued to do standard and long-wheelbase ambulance conversions of virtually any chassis preferred by the customer.

The fabulous 1950s went out with a real bang. Who can forget the high-finned '59s! America's funeral coach and ambulance makers faced a real design dilemma when they received the advance engineering drawings for the proposed 1959 Cadillac commercial chassis. Like all 1959 Cadillacs, the 1959 commercial chassis (redesignated the Series 6890) sported towering tailfins that looked more at home on a jet plane than on an automobile. Cadillac's gaudy tailfins—each skewered by dual taillight pods—marked the peak of 1950s automotive styling excess.

Perhaps better than any of its competitors, industry leader Superior rose to the challenge with not one but *two* series of dramatically styled new bodies for the high-finned 1959 Cadillac chassis. Like its '57s and '58s, Superior's 1959 ambulances and funeral coaches had sweeping, curved rooflines and huge glass areas. The new top-line Superior-Cadillac Crown Royale had forward-angled "C" pillars trimmed in bright chrome, which extended up across the car's roof. While decidedly flamboyant on funeral coaches, this dramatic new styling worked especially well on the company's limousine style ambulances and combination coaches—especially with the extruded aluminum lower body skeg moldings.

Miller-Meteor, Hess & Eisenhardt and Eureka all took more conservative approaches to their 1959 restyles. All 1959 Cadillac ambulances and combinations were knockouts and are eagerly sought by collectors today.

After a six-year absence The Flxible Company re-entered the funeral coach and ambulance business during the 1959 model year—again exclusively on Buick chassis. For

1954 Superior-Cadillac Moderne limousine combination funeral coach and ambulance. Note airline-type window drapes, removable "ambulance" insignia in rear side windows.

the first time, Flxible-Buick hearses, ambulances and combinations were available in two distinct sizes—the compact standard wheelbase Flxette and the long-wheelbase Premier. The Flxette picked up precisely where the Henney Junior had left off in 1954. The Flxette was built on the standard wheelbase Buick Electra chassis but with a raised greenhouse area and roof panel. The top-line Premier was a cut-and-splice job, just like Flxibles of old. Flxible did an outstanding job in designing dignified, clean-lined new bodies for the bat-winged 1959 Buick chassis.

There was more change among the struggling conversion builders. The former Guy Barnette Company was succeeded by a new entity, which marketed its product under a slightly different name—Barnett. In addition to Pontiacs, Barnett built at least one limousine combination on a 1959 Cadillac chassis. For 1959 the National Body Mfg. Company offered limousine and landau style funeral cars and ambulance conversions on all five General Motors passenger car chassis—Chevrolet, Pontiac, Oldsmobile, Buick and Cadillac. This would be the last year one could buy a new Comet funeral coach, ambulance or combination.

The Fabulous Fifties were winding down. Suddenly it was 1960.

Warning Devices

Mechanical coaster sirens reigned supreme as the emergency vehicle warning device of choice through the 1950s. No well-dressed ambulance was complete without an eye-catching (and ear-piercing) mechanical siren mounted on the roof or front fender. The siren itself was a chrome-plated work of art. The electric motor, rotor, etc., was encased in a streamlined, bullet-shaped, chrome-plated shell. Some sirens had a powerful flashing red light neatly integrated into the front of the unit, projecting both audio and visual warning signals.

The most popular sirens of the 1950s were Federal's mighty "Q," C-Series and smaller Model 66 and "W" Series sirens. For underhood mounting, Federal offered its models Q1 and 28. Federal's principal competitor was Sterling's familiar Model 20 and 30 Sirenlite. Other ambulance operators insisted on a B&M Super Chief or Siro-Drift. Competing siren makers still in business included Sireno and the H.O.R. Company, both located in Staten Island, New York, and C.A.M. in California.

With or without red lights, coaster sirens were often augmented by supplemental warning lights, such as the wig-wag Mars light or Federal's whirling Propello-Ray. Introduced in the late 1940s, Federal's Beacon-Ray had proved spectacularly successful with fire apparatus and ambulance manufacturers alike. Originally offered with two lamps, which rotated under a red plastic dome, a three-lamp Model 173 was added in the mid-1950s.

Premium model ambulances had bullet-shaped red and white warning lights faired into the front and rear of their raised roofs in addition to roof-mounted red beacons and coaster sirens. Demountable warning roof beacons, red lights mounted behind the grille, and underhood sirens were commonly used on combination coaches.

But a revolution in emergency vehicle warning devices was about to begin. The familiar rising-and-falling wail of the venerable coaster siren was about to be challenged by the programmable yelp, whoop and warble of the new *electronic* siren. Federal's breakthrough PA-1 had arrived

1954 S&S Cadillac high-headroom ambulance by Hess & Eisenhardt. Red Plexiglas panel at front of step roof was illuminated. Big rescue ambulances of this type could transport four patients with room for two attendants.

Studebaker marketed factory-built ambulances from 1954 to 1958. Attired in rescue squad uniform, Jeff Beyer shows off his 1955 Studebaker Commander Regal Ambulette at a Professional Car Society Meet.

1955 Miller-Cadillac ambulance owned by Dave Burkham of Decatur, Illinois. Distinctive "pinched" rear side windows were used on Miller-built professional cars from 1954 to 1956.

Three factory fresh 1954 Meteor-Cadillac ambulances lined up at the Meteor Motor Car Company plant in Piqua, Ohio. Ambulances, combinations and hearses in rear rows are 1953 models.

Phillip Jast brought this nicely equipped 1955 Superior-Cadillac "rescuer" ambulance to a 1989 PCS Meet. Note step-type roof, tunnel lights at all four corners and side flashers.

Exceptionally roomy Chevrolet and GMC panel vans were beginning to attract ambulance converters. Custom Body Service did this attractive ambulance conversion of a 1955 GMC 250.

Above. Economy Coach changed its name to Memphis Coach Company during the 1955 model year. The new company called its products "Memphians." Here is a 1955 Memphian-Pontiac limousine ambulance with trendy wraparound corner windows.

Left. Interior view of a 1955 Memphian-Pontiac ambulance showing two folding attendant's seats, stretcher locked in place.

1956 Memphian-Ford "Ambulette" conversion of Ford Courier sedan delivery. Note attractive two-tone paint, roof tunnel lights.

Meteor Motor Car Company offered flashy three-tone exterior color choices for 1956, as seen on this 1956 Meteor-Cadillac combination. This would be Meteor's final year.

The 1956 model year would also be the last for the A. J. Miller Company. PCS member Paul Vickery owns this nicely preserved 1956 Miller-Cadillac ambulance.

Comet Coach Company built hearses, ambulances and combinations mostly on Oldsmobile chassis between 1955 and 1959. This is the 1957 Comet-Oldsmobile 88 limousine combination.

National Body Manufacturing Company did hearse/ambulance conversions on any chassis desired by the customer. Among the most popular were 1955-1956-1957 National-Chevrolet "Minute Man" ambulances. Charles Havelka brought his 1956 National-Chevrolet to the 1995 PCS International Meet.

The Eureka Company built this impressive high-headroom ambulance on a 1957 Cadillac commercial chassis. Eureka called its hightop ambulances "Hi-Boys." Note flashing red lights at base of windshield, "ambulance" sign on dash.

Opposite page bottom. Rear view of 1956 Superior-Cadillac Moderne combination funeral coach/ambulance. Combinations were often painted neutral colors such as white, gray or blue for dual-duty.

Stylish standard-headroom 1957 Eureka-Cadillac ambulance restored by John R. Schmidt of Mount Lebanon, Pennsylvania.

All new Cadillac commercial chassis for 1957 permitted lower professional car bodies. Redesigned '57 Superior-Cadillacs boasted "Criterion" styling with thin rooflines, large glass area. This is a standard 42-inch Superior-Cadillac ambulance for 1957.

National Body Mfg. Co. offered Buick ambulances and combinations from 1954-1965. This rare 1957 National-Buick is owned by Ted and Susan Horning.

Newly formed Miller-Meteor division introduced its first professional cars for 1957. PCS member Dave McCamey of Berea, Ohio is the proud owner of this white-over-red 1957 Miller-Meteor Cadillac Classic Ambulance.

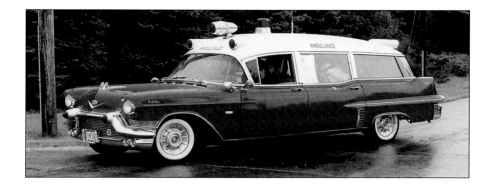

Rear view of Dave McCamey's 1957 Miller-Meteor Cadillac Classic Limousine Ambulance.

Dawson Blackmore's stunning white-over-red 1957 Memphian-DeSoto Ambulance turns heads wherever it goes. Memphis Coach Co. was mostly using Chrysler Corporation chassis at this time, including Dodge, DeSoto and Chrysler and even the odd Plymouth.

Rear view of Dawson Blackmore's 1957 Memphian-DeSoto Straight Ambulance. DeSoto Firedome's towering tailfins and two-tone paint scheme worked well with Memphian's limousine body design. Note high-base Beacon Ray in center of roof.

1957 Memphian-Chevrolet ambulance. Base car was a stripped-down Chevrolet 210. Tunnel lights house alternating red flashing lights.

All 1958 professional cars got new quad-headlights. This is a standard headroom 1958 Superior-Cadillac. Dual red tunnel lights match quad headlights.

1958 Superior-Pontiac combination funeral coach/ambulance on Bonneville chassis. Note step-type roof. Airline-type curtains could be drawn shut for privacy. Rear fender intake denotes an air-conditioned car.

Gene Griffith brought this 1958 Barnett-Pontiac combination to a 1992 PCS Meet in Lebanon, Missouri. "The fastest hearse in town," this coach was equipped with Pontiac's potent tri-carb V-8 engine option!

1959 Superior-Cadillac Royale Super Rescuer ambulance boasted 54 inches of rear compartment headroom. High-finned '59 commercial chassis made for some very flashy professional cars.

High-finned 1959 Cadillac professional cars are very desirable today. Flamboyant '59s—especially hearses—were of questionable taste when new. Dan Skivolocke's white-over-red 1959 Superior-Cadillac Royale 42-inch ambulance is a standout.

Hess & Eisenhardt (S&S) had more conservative 1959 body styling than rivals Superior and Eureka. This is the 1959 S&S Cadillac Kensington ambulance.

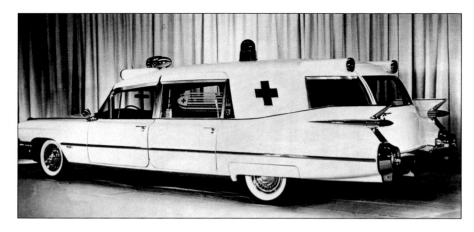

Miller-Meteor's top-line ambulance for 1959 was this distinctive M/M Ambulandau on a Cadillac chassis. Note large cross emblem on rear quarter panel.

Handsome white 1959 Eureka-Cadillac combination funeral coach and ambulance owned by Dan Brintlinger of Decatur, Illinois. Note split body side molding treatment.

Automotive Conversion Corporation specialized in ambulance and funeral car conversions of standard station wagons. ACC marketed an ambulance version of the Edsel Villager Wagon in 1958-1959. This is a 1959 Edsel Amblewagon.

Comet built one-off 1959 Chrysler Imperial hightop ambulance for Guy Mullen Company of St. Louis, Missouri. Called the "Blue Guardian," Mullen's custom-built Comet-Imperial sported B&M Super Chief siren on left front fender, Mars light on right. *Chrysler Historical Collection*

After six-year absence, Flxible re-entered the professional car market for 1959 — again exclusively on Buick chassis. This is the 1959 Flxible-Buick Premier combination. Flxible stylists did a commendable job with the bat-winged 1959 Buick chassis.

Interior view of 1959 Superior-Pontiac high-headroom ambulance outfitted to carry three patients. Note linoleum floor, four bullet lights over door.

1960 Miller-Meteor Cadillac "Volunteer" 48-inch headroom ambulance with red tunnel lights at all four corners. Steve Loftin owned this fine example.

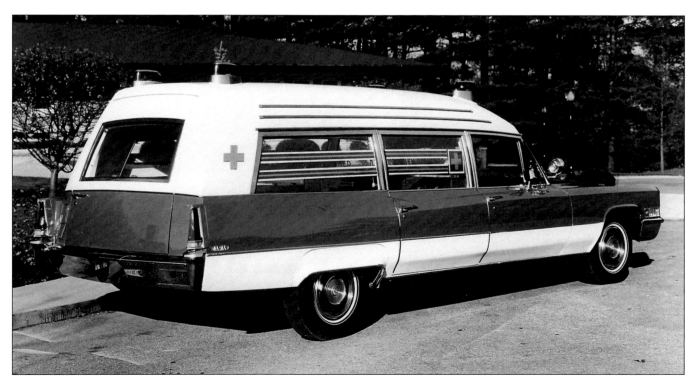

Factory photograph of a 1969 Miller-Meteor Cadillac Volunteer hightop ambulance. Note M/M "Full-Vu" lights at each corner.

The Sizzling Sixties 1960 - 1969

The 1960s marked yet another decade of growth, progress and prosperity for the American automobile industry and, similarly, for the thriving funeral coach and ambulance business. For the third consecutive decade, America continued to live in the shadow of war—this time a nationally-divisive conflict in far-off Vietnam.

The auto industry's 1960 models bowed with far more restrained styling than the gaudy 1959s. Tailfins were lower, body sides were cleaner and there was far less chrome. No better example of this welcome evolution could be found than on the 1960 Cadillacs. The rocketship fins of 1959 had receded into much lower, blade-like fins. Chrome trim was thin and sparingly applied—even on the finely textured new convex grille.

The 156-inch wheelbase Cadillac Series 6980 commercial chassis remained the backbone of the American professional car industry. Approximately three-quarters of the funeral coaches, ambulances, combinations and flower cars built in America rode on the special Cadillac hearse and ambulance chassis—just over 2,100 of which were produced for the 1960 model year.

There were some noteworthy changes among the smaller players in the industry this year. The Comet Coach Company of Blytheville, Arkansas, changed its name. The Ford Motor Company bought the Comet name for an undisclosed (presumably hefty) sum for use on a new Mercury compact passenger car to be introduced a few years later. The former Comet Coach Company's

1960 models were marketed under a new name—Cotner/Bevington. The company's new name was made up of those of the company's two founders, Waldo J. Cotner and Robert F. Bevington. The new Cotner/Bevington Corporation continued to specialize in long-wheelbase Oldsmobile funeral coaches, ambulances and combinations—although C/B (and predecessor Comet) also delivered some professional cars on Pontiac, Chevrolet and the occasional Buick chassis, including some raised-roof, short-wheelbase models.

Yet another new name joined the ever-changing roster of American professional car manufacturers this year. The Pinner Coach Company set up shop in Olive Branch, Mississippi, 10 miles south of Memphis, Tennessee. This new automotive enterprise bore the name of its founder and chief operating officer, Jack W. Pinner. The company's principal products were conservatively styled limousine combination coaches built on cut-and-stretched Pontiac Star Chief chassis—although Pinner also built some Chrysler and Ford-based units.

After a brief absence, The Shop of Siebert re-entered the ambulance and hearse business in 1960. Now located in Waterville, Ohio, a suburb of Toledo, Siebert introduced a new family of long-wheelbase hearses, ambulances and combination coaches built on stretched Ford chassis.

The base vehicle for these conversions, which were marketed as "Siebert Aristocrats," was the 1960 Ford Country Squire station wagon. These rather ungainly looking cars, with their high step-type roofs and distinctive trapezoid window center panels, utilized the standard station wagon doors requiring a long fillet extension between the rear door and the rear wheels.

The National Body Mfg. Company of Knightstown, Indiana, remained one of the busiest of the industry's second-tier players. National continued to construct ambulances, combinations and funeral cars on any chassis desired by the customer, including the odd Buick and Chrysler Imperial.

As the 1960s began, the U.S. hearse and ambulance industry was made up of 10 independent manufacturers—four of which built their funeral coaches, ambulances, combinations and flower cars on the Cadillac Series 8680 commercial chassis. They were:

- Superior Coach Corporation—Lima, Ohio
- Miller-Meteor Division, Piqua, Ohio
- The Hess & Eisenhardt Company—Cincinnati, Ohio
- The Eureka Company—Rock Falls, Illinois

These four long-established firms did the lion's share of the business. The rest of the professional car industry pie was divided up among six well-known *conversion* builders:

- The Flxible Company—Loudonville, Ohio
- National Body Mfg. Company—Knightstown, Indiana
- Cotner/Bevington Corporation—Blytheville, Arkansas
- Pinner Coach Company—Olive Branch, Mississippi
- The Shop of Siebert Associates—Waterville, Ohio
- Automotive Conversion Corporation—Birmingham, Michigan

Owned by Steve and Gene Lichtman of Mt. Airy, Maryland, this 1960 Flxible-Buick Premier ambulance once protected West Leechburg Works of the Allegheny Ludlum Steel Corporation.

Technically, Superior Coach Corporation's Southern Division in Kosiusko, Mississippi, should be included among the conversion builders, inasmuch as the Southern Division's output consisted entirely of hearse, ambulance, combination and funeral service car conversions of cut-and-spliced Pontiac Star Chief chassis.

In addition to these, any number of small local shops scattered across the country did ambulance conversions of their own utilizing small commercial-type vans, station wagons and vehicles like the International Travelall.

Superior Coach again marketed Cadillac ambulances in two series with three separate headrooms: the 42-inch Royale; the 48-inch Royale Rescuer and the 54-inch Super Rescuer. At the top of the line was the 48-inch Crowne Royale Rescuer.

Superior also continued to offer less expensive long-wheelbase Pontiac ambulances, with standard and 43-inch hightop roof configurations. Most Superior-Pontiacs, however, were still dual-purpose limousine style funeral coach and ambulance combinations.

At the end of the 1960 model year, Divco-Wayne transferred Miller-Meteor funeral coach and ambulance production from the A. J. Miller Company plant in Bellefontaine, Ohio, to the former Meteor Motor Car Company plant in Piqua, Ohio. The ancient A. J. Miller plant complex was closed.

The most unique ambulance design announced for 1960 was Miller-Meteor's imposing **Guardian**. Built on the Cadillac commercial chassis with 54 inches of headroom, the M/M Guardian's rear roof swept back to form a canopy that extended beyond the vehicle's large, flat rear door. The Miller-Meteor Guardian was intended for heavy-duty rescue service—fire departments, first-aid squads, etc. Few were sold, but the Guardian remained at the top of the Miller-Meteor Cadillac rescue-type ambulance lineup for the next three years.

Although the late, lamented Henney Motor Company had pioneered the short-wheelbase, raised-roof professional car in 1952, this type of vehicle did not really catch on in a big way until the 1960s. The "Henney Junior" on Packard Clipper chassis, was built from 1952 through the 1954 model year. The Flxible Company revived this concept with its standard-wheelbase Buick Flxette in 1959. In mid-1961 the Superior Coach Corporation announced its all-new Consort—a high-headroom professional car conversion based on the standard Pontiac Bonneville station wagon.

The all-new Superior-Pontiac Consort was available as a straight ambulance, a combination funeral coach/ambulance or as a landau-style hearse or service car.

Superior's top-line ambulance for 1960 was this Cadillac 54-inch headroom ""Super Rescuer." Note linen and medicine cabinet behind driver's seat.

93

The compact Consort nicely complemented Superior's long-wheelbase Pontiacs and commercial chassis Cadillacs.

The Cotner/Bevington Corporation also moved into the compact coach field this year. Based on the 123-inch wheelbase Oldsmobile 88, the 1961 Cotner/Bevington Oldsmobile Seville would soon prove to be one of the company's most popular products. The long-wheelbase Cotner/Bevington Oldsmobiles were called C/B Cotingtons. The most prolific of these were limousine style combination coaches with airline-type window curtains.

Richard Brothers of Eaton Rapids, Michigan, announced a new raised-roof version of the 1961 Chrysler New Yorker or Newport Town & Country station wagon. With six inches of added headroom, the all-new second-generation Chrysler Briarean was available as a funeral coach, an ambulance or as a combination funeral coach/ambulance. The Briarean retained the Chrysler four-door hardtop station wagon's window configuration but was fitted with a one-piece raised roof panel. Rear window drapes on all models were of the classic "airline"-type.

The Flxible Company introduced an ingenious dual-latching system option for its 1962 Buick professional cars. Flxible's "Flxi-Door" rear door could be opened from either the right or left. The sight of door handles on

each side of the rear door must have been puzzling to other drivers following a Flxible down the road!

Superior Coach provided two special 1962 Cadillac Super Rescuer 48-inch High Headroom Ambulances for the 1962 World's Fair in Seattle. Hess & Eisenhardt introduced its Custom Professional Parkway hightop ambulance. Miller-Meteor built its last Guardian rescue ambulance this year—and Richard Brothers discontinued its second-generation Chrysler Briarean after only two years.

In 1963, the Miller-Meteor Division of the Divco-Wayne Corporation edged past Superior Coach to become the largest player in the hearse and ambulance industry. These two giants would engage in a seesaw battle for industry leadership for years to come.

There were two milestone developments in the industry in 1964. First, Wayne Works acquired its **third** professional car manufacturer. The Wayne conglomerate had earlier purchased Meteor and Miller, which it merged to form Miller-Meteor. Wayne's latest acquisition was the Cotner/Bevington Corporation. The moderately priced Cotner/Bevington Oldsmobiles nicely complemented M/M's top-line Cadillacs and gave M/M dealers something with which to compete with Superior's Pontiacs and Flxible's Buicks. Cotner/Bevington Oldsmobile production,

1960 Superior-Cadillac Crown Royale limousine combination funeral coach and ambulance, Feller-Graffs Funeral Home, Waterloo, Indiana.

Siebert continued to offer truck-based ambulance conversions. This stretched 1960 Ford panel served Millgrave, New York Volunteer Fire Department.

Gorgeous 1961 Eureka-Cadillac combination funeral coach and ambulance owned by Bill Marcy, Hackensack, New Jersey.

Attractive 1961 Flxible-Buick Flxette landau ambulance. Compact Flxette was built on standard passenger car wheelbase.

Tom Parkinson photographed this rare Memphian-bodied 1961 Pontiac hightop ambulance in Berkeley, California.

Springfield Equipment Company marketed popular ambulance conversions of the International Travelall. Champion's Interne rode on a 140-inch wheelbase. This 1964 Springfield/International served Edina, Minnesota, Fire Department.

Superior Coach built this special 1962 Rescuer 48-inch hightop ambulance on a Cadillac commercial chassis for the "Century 21" exposition in Seattle, Washington.

Superior announced compact Pontiac Consort in mid-1961. Built on Pontiac station wagon chassis, Consort was offered through 1973. Here's a military spec 1962 Superior-Pontiac Consort ambulance.

however, remained at the Blytheville, Arkansas, plant.

The other milestone event this year was the disappearance of one of the industry's oldest and most respected names. The Eureka Company quietly ceased professional car production at the end of the 1964 model year, unable to absorb the very high cost of engineering and developing new professional car bodies for the all-new 1965 Cadillac commercial chassis. Incorporated in 1887, Eureka had been in business for 77 years—47 of them as a senior member of the U.S. hearse and ambulance industry.

The all-new 1965 Cadillac commercial chassis marked the biggest change since Cadillac had introduced its "X"-frame hearse/ambulance chassis eight years earlier. Cadillac's totally-redesigned Series 69890 commercial chassis was of a new "box perimeter frame" design. Wheelbase remained at 156 inches. The demise of Eureka left Cadillac with only three customers for this chassis—Superior, Miller-Meteor and Hess & Eisenhardt.

The industry lost yet another veteran member in 1965. The Flxible Company again decided to get out of the hearse and ambulance business—this time for good. Although the company had constructed prototypes of its 1965 Flxette and Premier professional cars (on Buick Wildcat instead of Electra chassis) they never went into production at Loudonville.

Flxible sold its Buick professional car tooling to the National Body Mfg. Company of Knightstown, Indiana. National built a number of these Flxible-designed National-Buicks during the 1965 model year.

In terms of production volume, one of the industry's most active "independents" was the Automotive Conversion Corporation of Birmingham, Michigan. This company had been successfully marketing ambulance and funeral service car conversions of standard passenger station wagons since 1955. ACC offered funeral directors a wide range of equipment to convert factory-built GM, Ford, Chrysler and AMC station wagons into hard-working ambulances or combinations. These conversions ranged all the way from the simple installation of a cot lock and removable "Ambulance" rear side window panels to a completely dressed and equipped Amblewagon Ambulance or Arlington hearse. The company's staple products were economy-model ambulances. After a few years of service the ambulance or funeral car equipment could be easily removed and the station wagon sold on the public used car market.

Yet another new professional car builder arrived on the scene in 1967. The Trinity Coach Company set up shop in Duncanville,

Miller-Meteor's top rescue-type ambulance was the high-headroom Guardian built between 1960 and 1962. Guardian had distinctive rear roof canopy, flat rear door. This is a 1962 M/M Cadillac Guardian.

Texas. Trinity Coach began production of standard and extended-wheelbase Buick ambulances, combinations and funeral coaches. Trinity's standard wheelbase model was called the Trinity Triune. Long-wheelbase models were called Trinity Royals. Alas, Trinity was to be short-lived. The company went out of business after only two years. There would be no 1969 Trinity-Buicks.

Among the smaller players, Pinner Coach was hanging right in there with the big boys, occasionally turning out custom-built hightop ambulances on Cadillac chassis.

Major changes were in the offing. After many years of ownership by the Shields family, the Superior Coach Corporation was sold in 1968 to the Sheller-Globe Corporation. Huge industrial conglomerates now owned the industry's two largest players.

As the 1960s wound down, winds of change were blowing over the ambulance manufacturing business as it had existed for the previous four decades. Ambulance conversions of compact light-duty vans like the Ford Econoline, GMC Carry-All and Chevrolet Suburban were winning increasing acceptance among ambulance operators and funeral directors. Although these truck-based ambulances lacked the soft ride and the pizzazz of the big Cadillacs, they offered far more interior room than passenger car-based units. And they were affordable. The light-duty van and truck conversions were price-competitive with the less-expensive Pontiac and Oldsmobile units.

Not all of these new ventures were suc-cessful. In the early 1960s, Ambulance Imports, Inc. of Warsaw, Indiana, began marketing Mercedes-Benz ambulances imported from Germany in the U.S. Built by Miesen of Bonn, these Mercedes-Benz 190 straight ambulances were significantly shorter—and taller—than their American counterparts. Despite their obvious high quality and practicality, few of these European prototype ambulances were sold here.

National (now reorganized as National Custom Coaches) stopped building passenger car-based professional cars altogether to concentrate on volume production of Chevrolet Suburban ambulances. Miller-Meteor and Cotner/Bevington's parent company was bolstering its Oldsmobile and Cadillac ambulance sales with an increasingly popular Chevrolet Suburban ambulance conversion called the Wayne Sentinel.

In November 1965, Robert H. Kennedy, M.D., then Director of the American College of Surgeons' Field Committee on Trauma, addressed the annual convention of the American Funeral Directors Association in Chicago. Dr. Kennedy noted that more than 50 percent of the ambulances in service in the United States were still owned and operated by local funeral directors. Of the more than 100,000 lives lost in accidents annually, he said, it was estimated that as many as 20,000 might be saved through improved first-aid, ambulance care and emergency department treatment. Clearly, something better was needed.

This fire engine red 1961 Siebert-Ford Aristocrat Hightop Ambulance originally served a New Jersey fire company first-aid squad. Base vehicle for this ambitious stretch conversion was a 1961 Ford Country Squire Station Wagon.

Warning Devices

Just as the electric siren had replaced bells and gongs in the 1920s, the electronic siren all but revolutionized emergency vehicle warning signals during the 1960s. Federal's pioneering PA-1 was soon joined by improved versions—the PA-15 and PA-20—and a host of competitors.

The first electronic sirens projected their variable sound patterns through a single, wide-mouthed flat-topped speaker, which closely resembled a standard public address system speaker. The new electronic sirens—usually mounted on the roof of the car—also had an extremely useful built-in PA speaker through which amplified messages or orders could be broadcast via a hand-held microphone from inside the car. A dial permitted the operator to choose from several distinctly different siren tones—continuous wail, yelp, bark or stutter—or the public address function at the accident or fire scene.

With the arrival of the new electronic sirens, the tried-and-true mechanical siren that had dominated the warning signal industry for more than 40 years began to fade from the scene. Well-maintained coaster sirens were routinely transferred from the old ambulance to the new one, sometimes serving on a dozen or more cars.

Now they were disconnected, unbolted and stored in the back room with outdated cots, stretchers, resuscitators and other castoff ambulance equipment. One notable exception was Federal's extremely popular "Q." This distinctive mechanical siren (Q2B with siren brake) continued to occupy a place of prominence on the roofs of ambulances of all types.

Another trend that emerged in the 1960s was the use of more than one beacon light on the same car. Typically, beacon lights were mounted on each side of the roof, above the front doors. Federal also introduced new, improved versions of its popular Beacon Ray. New models featured red **and** white lamps under a clear plastic dome. The pulsating combination of flashing red and white lights proved an effective traffic-buster.

Capitalizing on this growing trend, Federal introduced its Model 11 Twin Beacon Ray in 1962. This unit consisted of a pair of outboard-mounted beacon lights with two CP25 siren/speakers mounted in the center of the assembly. Federal's "Visibar" was designed to attach to the roof rain gutters of a standard passenger car. Six years later this company advanced its "light bar" concept with the Model 12 Twin Sonic, on which lights and speaker were housed in a full-width plastic housing.

Deluxe hightop ambulances often had an illuminated "Ambulance" sign or the operator's name built into the leading edge of the step-type fiberglass roof panel, and on similarly illuminated side panels.

Cotner-Bevington's entry into the short-wheelbase professional car market was with the C/B Seville. Shown is Joe Ortiz's 1962 Cotner/Bevington/Oldsmobile Seville ambulance with Mars "football" light at Southern California Chapter PCS Meet.

Long-wheelbase Cotner/Bevington/Oldsmobiles were called Cotingtons. This rare 1961 Cotner/Bevington/Oldsmobile Cotington 46-inch hightop ambulance saw service in New Jersey.

Best known for its Oldsmobiles, Cotner-Bevington built some Chevrolet and Pontiac ambulances, too. This 1962 Cotner/Bevington/Chevrolet short-wheelbase combination attended the 1995 PCS International Meet.

Richard Brothers of Eaton Rapids, Michigan marketed Chrysler-based, raised-roof Brierian combinations. This baby blue 1962 Chrysler New Yorker Brierian ambulance served Almond, New York.

McClintock Manufacturing specialized in Chrysler sedan ambulance conversions in the 1950s. Mike Reifer owns this very unusual 1962 McClintock/Chrysler side-loading sedan ambulance with dual Federal C6BR sirens!

Standard 42-inch headroom 1963 Superior-Cadillac Royale limousine ambulance photographed at Lima, Ohio plant. Black side-wall tires are unusual.

1963 Miller-Meteor Cadillac Volunteer 48-inch hightop ambulance used by the East Detroit Fire Department. Warning lights include four M/M Full-Vu lights at corners, Federal beacon ray in center of roof.

Siebert re-entered the professional car market in 1960. Bob Collier of Fremont, Ohio owns this nicely restored 1963 Siebert-Ford Aristocrat ambulance which originally served Springfield Township, Ohio.

For every big Cadillac ambulance out there, dozens of less glamorous station wagon conversions were saving lives, too. Bob Taber's home-built 1963 Chevrolet Biscayne ambulance served Macedon, New York.

Pinner Coach Company specialized in limousine style combinations. Here's a classic 1963 Pinner-Pontiac combination with airline style drapes.

Rick Duffy's impressive 1964 Miller-Meteor Cadillac Volunteer 42-inch ambulance. Note distinctive M/M "Full-Vu" corner lights, Federal Strato-ray beacon.

Rear view of crisp-lined 1964 Miller-Meteor Cadillac Duplex limousine combination then owned by Jerry McClure. Body color is Nevada Silver.

1964 Miller-Meteor Cadillac Paramount combination hearse/ambulance. Note high-base roof beacon, clear Plexiglas "ambulance" sign in window.

Business end of a 1964 S&S Cadillac Superline Parkway ambulance. Stretcher is locked in place on left, two folding attendant's seats on right.

1964 Superior-Pontiac 46-inch hightop ambulance custom built for Kingwood rescue squad. Note big bullet lights above rear door.

Shortly after the start of the 1965 model year, Flxible sold its professional car tooling to National Body Manufacturing Company of Knightstown, Indiana. Tim Fantin owns this 1965 National-Buick combination on a Buick Wildcat chassis.

Another 1965 National-Buick ambulance, this one on a Buick Electra 225 chassis. Bob Hedges brought this bright white car to a 1993 PCS Meet. Note Fireball light on dash.

A popular participant at PCS International Meets is Robert F. Parsons' 1965 Superior-Cadillac 42-inch ambulance. Note Superior bullet lights, fender-mounted "888s", Federal "Q" siren concealed behind grille.

Opposite page bottom. 1964 Cotner/Bevington/Oldsmobile Cotington combination owned by John Wurm, Forest Lake, Minnesota. Note airline style window curtains, removable "ambulance" panels in rear side windows.

1965 S&S Cadillac Park Row limousine combination funeral coach/ambulance in funeral service trim. Note distinctive S&S trim on front of hood. S&S used airline-type curtains between 1954 and 1970.

A 1966 Superior-Cadillac Royale Rescuer 48-inch ambulance with Premium trim. Note illuminated name panel, roof vent, high-base beacon and Federal Solarays on both front fenders.

Prototypical 1966 Superior-Cadillac Royale Landaulet combination funeral coach/ambulance. Identifying giveaways are airline-type drapes, dual roof beacons and spotlights.

Nifty 1966 Superior-Pontiac Consort combination owned by William R. Deegan, Pottstown, Pennsylvania. Note "Tiara" trim treatment on rear roof area.

1966 Cotner/Bevington/Oldsmobile 48-inch hightop ambulance owned by John Wurm, Forest Lake, Minnesota.

1967 S&S Cadillac professional high body ambulance in service with Wellsboro, Pennsylvania Fire Department. Busy roof sports Federal C6 siren, Solarays in tunnels, red-faced unity spotlights.

Fine Steve Lichtman portrait of a 1967 S&S Cadillac professional high body ambulance at a PCS International Meet. Tunnel lights over cab house red Solarays.

1967 Superior-Pontiac 48-inch hightop ambulance photographed against a backdrop of Kaiser Jeep Gladiator M725 military ambulances at the Superior Coach plant in Lima, Ohio.

Ted Kalinowski portrait of a standard 1967 Superior-Pontiac 48-inch hightop ambulance at a Kitchener, Ontario fire apparatus muster.

Ambulance assembly line in Superior's southern division plant in Kosiusko, Missouri. Cadillacs were built in Superior's home plant in Lima, Ohio. We count eight 1967 Superior-Pontiacs under construction.

National built its last passenger car-type ambulances in 1967 and 1968 before switching to Chevrolet Suburban conversions exclusively. This is a 1967 National-Chrysler built off Flxible tooling.

1967 Superior-Cadillac Royale 42-inch limousine ambulance. Note pair of chrome-plated CP25 siren speakers mounted on front fenders, two big Federal 184 flattop beacons on roof.

Bob Clifford of Allison Park, Pennsylvania is the proud owner of this beautifully restored 1967 Superior-Cadillac Sovereign Tiara limousine combination.

A nicely restored 1968 S&S Cadillac Park Row ambulance owned by John Rabold, South Bend, Indiana. Photographed at a recent PCS International Meet.

The short-lived Trinity Coach Company of Duncanville, Texas built Buick ambulances and funeral coaches in 1967 and 1968. This short-wheelbase 1968 Trinity-Buick Triune ambulance is owned by well-known movie car supplier Joe Ortiz, Shadow Hills, California.

Long-wheelbase Trinity Buicks were called Trinity Royals. Bobb R. Koboff of Littlerock, California owned this sharp two-toned 1968 Trinity-Buick Royal straight ambulance.

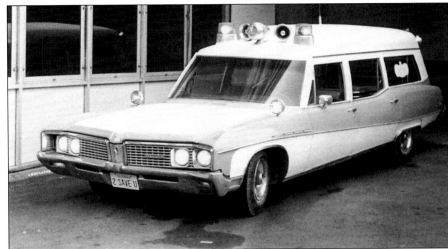

Pinner Coach built some Cadillac ambulances. Note Solaray tunnel lights, Dietz 211 beacon and six clearance lights on leading edge of step-type roof on this 1968 Pinner-Cadillac.

1969 Superior-Cadillac Sovereign limousine combination owned by Paul Saether, Blanchardville, Wisconsin. Combination coaches usually had front-hinged rear side doors. Note air-conditioning vent on rear fender.

Detroit Fire Commissioner Paxton Mendelssohn donated this huge mobile medical unit to the Detroit Fire Department in 1968. Unit 300 was built by Gerstenslager on GMC truck chassis.

More hearse than ambulance is this 1969 Miller-Meteor Cadillac classic limousine combination with removable landau panels, roof beacons in place for funeral service.

Some ambulance collectors like to load up on lights. John Klein's 1969 Miller-Meteor Cadillac Volunteer sports #184 beacon, Federal "Q," dual Mars 888s, CP25 speakers, red and white grille lights.

1969 Cotner/Bevington/Oldsmobile Seville straight ambulance. Note "lollipop" lights on roof, high-base beacon, Federal "Q," unorthodox red lights on front fenders.

Despite electronic revolution, some ambulance operators still preferred big coaster sirens. This 1969 Superior-Pontiac 48-inch hightop sports a lusty Federal C6.

The look of the future! Ford profoundly affected ambulance design with the introduction of all-new full-size vans in 1968. Ontario (Canada) Hospital Services Commission used this early 1969 Ford van ambulance conversion.

Hess & Eisenhardt's standard-headroom ambulance was the 42.5-inch S&S Parkway. This 1970 S&S Cadillac Parkway served Adams-Hanover Patient Services in Bonneauville, Pennsylvania.

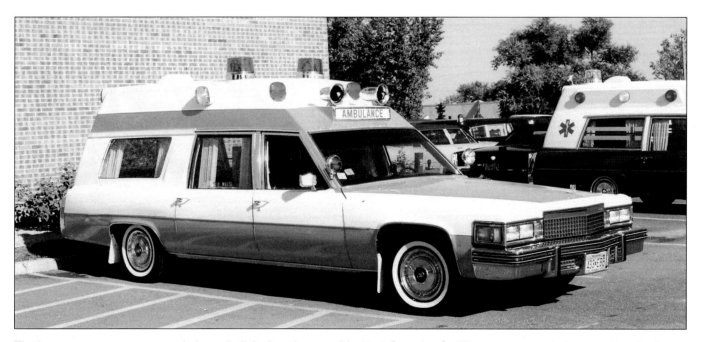

The last passenger car-type ambulance built in America was this 1979 Superior-Cadillac transport ambulance sold to Dr. Roger D. White of Rochester, Minnesota. Milestone Ambulance participated in the 1996 Twin Cities' PCS International Meet.

End of an Era
1970 - 1979

Although few would have predicted it as the decade began, the final years of the 1970s would be the most tumultuous for the long-established American ambulance manufacturers since the automobile replaced the horse. By the end of the decade, the passenger car-based ambulance and the dual-purpose combination coach would be virtually regulated out of existence.

For the parent automobile industry, the early- to mid-1970s was marked by a series of Mid-East oil scares, frightening national fuel shortages, long lines at the gasoline pumps and—consequently—the federally-mandated "downsizing" of all U.S. passenger cars.

The auto industry wasn't the only business impacted by burgeoning government regulation. Sweeping new federal standards, which for the first time regulated ambulance design, equipment carried and—most importantly—the training and qualifications of the men and women who manned them, would ultimately displace the soft-riding, luxury passenger car-type ambulance, which had been the accepted standard of emergency patient transport in America for nearly three-quarters of a century.

The decade certainly *began* normally enough. The Cadillac commercial chassis remained the backbone of the U.S. hearse and ambulance industry which was now dominated by two major players—both owned by huge, diversified industrial conglomerates, and the last of the small, independent funeral coach and ambulance manufacturers.

The *passenger car-based* hearse and ambulance industry now included only five players—*half as many* as it had a decade earlier. Here's what the industry looked like as the 1970s began:

- Miller-Meteor Division of Divco-Wayne Corporation
- Superior Division of Sheller-Globe, Inc.
- Cotner/Bevington Division of Divco-Wayne
- The Hess & Eisenhardt (S&S) Company

Remarkably, there was just **one** of the old-line conversion builders left. The Automotive Conversion Corporation, which had relocated to Troy, Michigan, continued to turn out Amblewagon ambulance and funeral car conversions of standard station wagons and, increasingly, ambulance conversions of vans and Suburbans.

Over the previous three years a number of **new** names—Horton, Springfield and Modular among them—had sprung up and were doing a booming business turning out practical, price-competitive ambulances on light-duty truck chassis. It is important to note that these new enterprises built ambulances and ambulances **only**—they did **not** make funeral coaches or combinations. The handwriting was clearly on the wall.

As they had for decades, Miller-Meteor, Superior and S&S continued to build and market passenger car-based ambulances as a profitable sideline to their core hearse-manufacturing business. A significant number of their funeral coach customers continued to provide ambulance service to their communities—thus the dual-purpose Combination Funeral Coach/Ambulance remained one of the most popular models in every manufacturer's professional car lineup.

For 1970, all three of these companies continued to offer entire *families* of ambulances on the 1970 Cadillac Series 69890 commercial chassis. These would remain in production through the middle of the decade. Here's what the professional ambulance operator or funeral director could choose from this year:

Superior-Cadillac: 42-inch standard headroom and 51- and 54-inch high-headroom ambulances; 40-, 48- and 51-inch headroom long-wheelbase Superior-Pontiacs and the 40-inch regular wheelbase Pontiac Consort Ambulance.

Miller-Meteor offered a 42-inch Guardian, a 48-inch Volunteer, a 50-inch Interceptor and a 54-inch headroom Lifeliner, all on Cadillac commercial chassis. Sister division Cotner/Bevington weighed in with 42- and 48-inch headroom long-wheelbase Cotington Oldsmobiles and the standard wheelbase 41-inch C/B Seville.

Hess and Eisenhardt continued to offer a choice of three luxurious Cadillac-chassised ambulances; the 42.5-inch standard headroom S&S Parkway; the 50-inch S&S Kensington and, at the top of the line, the impressive 54-inch S&S Professional High Body.

Make no mistake about it, these firms were by no means oblivious to what was happening in the ambulance-manufacturing business beyond their own factory walls. In the late 1960s, Wayne Corporation, which owned Miller-Meteor and Cotner/Bevington, had introduced a Chevrolet Suburban ambulance called the Wayne Sentinel. Superior Coach had entered the fray with a factory-built ambulance conversion of the roomy Ford Econoline Van. These new vehicles were finding a lot of new customers.

Cadillac introduced a major restyle for 1971, but a prolonged strike at General Motors during the last quarter of 1970 delayed volume deliveries of the new 1971 commercial chassis until early 1971. Superior, Miller-Meteor and S&S all introduced restyled hearse and ambulance bodies for this handsome new chassis with its long hood and widely spaced square headlight bezels. Changes for 1972 were pretty much cosmetic. The 1973 commercial chassis, however, was equipped with GM's new energy-absorbing front bumper system. The grille assembly retracted with the bumper in low-speed impacts, minimizing front-end damage.

By 1974, all three makers of Cadillac ambulances had added extra-heavy duty rescue-type ambulances to the top of their product lines. Superior announced its big 54XL. Miller-Meteor leapfrogged its own Lifeliner with the new Criterion, and Hess & Eisenhardt countered with its impressive Medic Mark 1.

The 1975-1976 Cadillac ambulances were the last of the really *big* ones. Powered by Cadillac's 500-cubic-inch (8.0 liter) V8

John Rabold's 1970 Miller-Meteor Cadillac classic limousine combination funeral coach/ambulance. White was a popular color for dual-purpose combination coaches.

engine, the 1975-1976 CZ90 commercial chassis sported square headlight units, which wrapped in a continuous band around the front corners of the car into the turn and parking lights. The 1976 model year was one of the best in the industry's history as funeral directors and ambulance operators stocked up on traditional full-sized ambulances and funeral coaches while they were still available.

During the 1960s and 1970s, several companies attempted to market—with limited success—innovative new ambulance adaptations of various other types of vehicles including package delivery vans, the Checker Marathon taxi (Checker MediCruiser)—and even recreational vehicle motor homes.

Hess & Eisenhardt introduced one of the most impressive of the latter in the early

This 50-inch headroom 1970 Miller-Meteor Cadillac Interceptor enjoyed a second career at Hagerstown Speedway after retirement by Clear Spring, Maryland.

Profile portrait of Dan Brintlinger's award winning 1970 Miller-Meteor Cadillac 48-inch Volunteer ambulance by Ted Kalinowski. Note roof-mounted Federal "Q" siren, Full-Vu 360-degree corner lights and big flattop beacon.

1970s. The H & E "Para Medic" EMS Ambulance was based on the fiberglass-bodied, tandem-axle, front-wheel-drive GMC motor home. H & E's big GMC Para Medic was powered by a 455-cubic-inch V8 engine. With 6.5 feet of headroom and 16 feet of rear compartment space, Hess & Eisenhardt noted that the Para Medic was just a foot longer and higher than the company's largest S&S Cadillac ambulance. EVF, Inc. of Riviera Beach, Florida, also offered a Mobile Intensive Care Unit on this sleek GMC RV chassis. Grumman's Emergency Vehicles Division later introduced a similar type of Super Ambulance, and a number of big Cortez motor homes were also converted into special-purpose medical units.

The oil scares of 1973 and 1974-1975 had had a chilling effect on the U.S. auto industry. Overnight, market demand for small cars skyrocketed while the big, gas-hungry V8s Americans had always loved languished on dealer lots. Faced with tough, new corporate average fuel economy (CAFÉ) standards, the Big Three (and American Motors, too) auto companies knuckled down to design, develop and place into production an entirely new generation of smaller, lighter, more fuel-efficient cars.

Stepping up to the plate, industry leader General Motors pledged to "downsize" all of its full-sized passenger cars for the 1977 model year. And downsize they did. The 1977 Chevrolets, Pontiacs, Oldsmobiles, Buicks and Cadillacs were all significantly smaller, lighter and more fuel-efficient than the 1976 models which they replaced. Ford and Chrysler soon followed suit.

While this massive vehicle downsizing marked a turning point in U.S. auto industry history, this transition had an absolutely devastating effect on the much smaller—and more vulnerable—professional car industry.

Along with its Chevys, Oldsmobiles and Cadillacs, General Motors also downsized its 1977 Cadillac hearse and ambulance chassis. Wheelbase of the all-new Series 69890 commercial chassis was shortened by 13.2 inches—from 157.5 inches in 1976 to 144.3 inches for 1977. With simultaneous new model launches at all of its large car plants, GM was unable to commence deliveries of the new 1977 commercial chassis until late in the 1976 calendar year.

Funeral directors and ambulance operators balked at paying significantly higher prices for smaller vehicles—*more money for less car.* Combined 1977 model year production by the three principal funeral coach and ambulance manufacturers (Superior, M/M and S&S) plunged to less than 1,300 vehicles compared with the well over 2,000 they previously built and sold annually. This situation would deteriorate even further over the next two years. Cadillac shipped just 852 commercial chassis during the 1978 model year, and an incrementally higher 864 in 1979.

The ambulance side of the professional car industry was especially hard-hit. The Federal Government's tough new "KKK" ambulance specifications gave Superior, M/M and Hess & Eisenhardt a massive disincentive to continue to build and market passenger car-based ambulances.

When the downsized 1977 professional cars were announced to the trade in the fall of 1976, Superior and Miller-Meteor each listed only *one* Cadillac-chassised ambulance in their sharply reduced product lines. Both were step-roof hightops. Hess & Eisenhardt discontinued ambulance production altogether. The last S&S Cadillac ambulance was delivered at the end of the 1976 model year.

Superior, meanwhile, had discontinued Pontiac funeral coach and ambulance production at the end of the 1975 model year. Cotner/Bevington went out of business at about the same time.

Superior and Miller-Meteor didn't even start producing their new ambulances until early in 1977. Production volume was miniscule by previous standards. The downsized high-headroom ambulances weren't even promoted as rescue or emergency-type ambulances—they were now classified as simply "transport" ambulances, designed primarily to transport non-emergency patients, just as the "Invalid Coach" had half a century earlier!

Both Miller-Meteor and Superior continued to offer combination coaches on the new downsized chassis—but there were now few customers for them. The new KKK regulations had effectively barred the use of ambulances as hearses, and vice versa. After decades of service to their communities, many funeral directors sold off their ambulance operations or got out of the ambulance business altogether.

Long the bread-and-butter car of every professional car manufacturer's product line, the classic dual-purpose combination was about to go the way of the Edsel.

Superior built only 10 of its downsized ambulances in each of the 1977, 1978 and 1979 model years. Miller-Meteor built even fewer. Industry volume had plunged to a fraction of what it had been only a few years earlier. Superior Coach built the last passenger car-type Cadillac-chassised ambulance at the end of the 1979 model year. The passenger car-based ambulance had suddenly come to the end of the road.

This situation went from bad to worse. In a surprise announcement, Miller-Meteor went out of business at the end of the 1979 model year. Late in 1980, Sheller-Globe abruptly shut down Superior Coach. A group of loyal longtime Superior employees acquired the name and assets and formed a new company, Superior Coaches, which resumed Cadillac funeral coach production (but not ambulances) at a much smaller facility in Lima in mid-1981. Later that year Hess & Eisenhardt sold its S&S funeral coach division to longtime rival Superior.

A new company in Toronto, Ontario, resurrected the Eureka name in 1981. The Miller-Meteor name was also revived in the 1980s. None of these latter-day reincarnations, however, ever built an ambulance.

The passenger car-type ambulance was now a relic of the past. But through all this industry turmoil and upheaval, the van and modular ambulance business was booming. Read on.

Andy Toton's 1970 Miller-Meteor Cadillac combination funeral coach/ambulance. Note color-coordinated removable landau panels, red-faced unity spotlights, Federal #17 beacon ray on roof.

Standard-wheelbase Seville was Cotner/Bevington's answer to rival Superior's Pontiac Consort. Light metallic blue 1970 Cotner/Bevington/Oldsmobile Seville combination with black crinkle roof dressed for ambulance duty.

Warning Devices

Electronic sirens, light bars, pulsating strobe lights and—to a lesser extent—air horns had all but replaced mechanical sirens (but not quite entirely) and red lights on emergency vehicles of all types. The major players in the increasingly competitive emergency signal industry were Federal Sign & Signal, Whelen, Code 3, Sireno, Fyr Fyter—and even gun maker Smith & Wesson.

The typical passenger car-type ambulance of this era typically sported one or more roof-mounted beacons, a roof-mounted Federal "Q" or other mechanical siren or a pair of chrome-plated siren speakers, or one of the many electronic siren/light combinations now available.

In 1977, Federal introduced its Model 24 AeroDynic, a contoured, aerodynamically designed light bar.

The DOT meanwhile had issued its own specifications for the mounting of warning lights, reflectors, etc. on the increasingly popular van and modular-type ambulances. Red, amber, white and blue lights, reflectors and warning signals had to be mounted in specific locations to meet visibility requirements of FMVSS 108 and the new KKK-A-1822 ambulance specifications. These included the sides and rear of the vehicle as well as the roof and grille areas.

Rear view of 1970 Superior-Pontiac 48-inch hightop ambulance. White-over-red was a very popular color scheme for straight ambulances like this one.

Wayne Corporation introduced the Chevrolet Suburban-based Sentinel ambulance in 1969. Jim Eaton brought his very original white-over-red 1970 Wayne Sentinel to a PCS International Meet. Note Federal combination electronic siren/beacon on roof.

1971 Superior-Cadillac Sovereign Regency combination operated by Bettschen & Daughter Funeral Service, Beach Park, Illinois. Note red inboard headlights.

Introduced in 1970, Miller-Meteor's top-line ambulance got a new name—Lifeliner. California Chapter PCS member Jim Crabtree drove his big 1971 Miller-Meteor Cadillac Lifeliner cross-country to a PCS Meet in Lancaster, Pennsylvania.

Rear view of Jim Crabtree's authentically equipped 1971 Miller-Meteor Cadillac Lifeliner. Miller-Meteor's flagship ambulance boasted 54 inches of patient compartment headroom.

Hess & Eisenhardt's most prestigious hightop ambulance also got a new name—Medic Mark 1. Evan J. Butchers of Frankford, Ontario, Canada is the proud owner of this 1971 S&S Cadillac Medic Mark 1, which originally served Myerstown, Pennsylvania.

Rear-view mirror view of Evan Butchers' 1971 S&S Medic Mark 1. Lots of red lights, Federal Visibar and illuminated red plastic "ambulance" name panel on front of raised roof.

Automotive Conversion Corporation continued to offer Amblewagon ambulance conversions of standard station wagons. Bob Dudley of Suffield, Ohio owns this bright red 1971 Ford Country Squire Amblewagon ambulance with loaded light bar.

Modular Ambulance Corporation built Chevrolet Suburban-based ambulances as well as modular units. This 1971 Chevrolet "Modulance" served Vaughn, New Mexico.

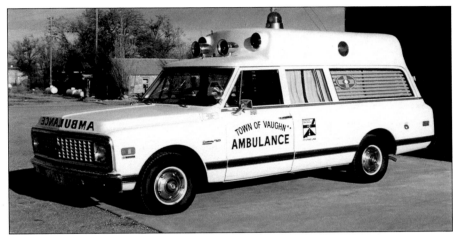

Miller-Meteor's standard-headroom Cadillac ambulance for 1972 was the Guardian 42. This very original white-over-orange 1972 M/M Guardian is owned by Jeff Glancy of Montpelier, Indiana. Note red lenses on inboard headlights, which flashed alternately.

A glossy black-over-white 1972 Superior-Pontiac Consort limousine combination once operated by Smith Funeral Home, Sapulpa, Oklahoma. The short-wheelbase Consort was offered from 1961 to 1973.

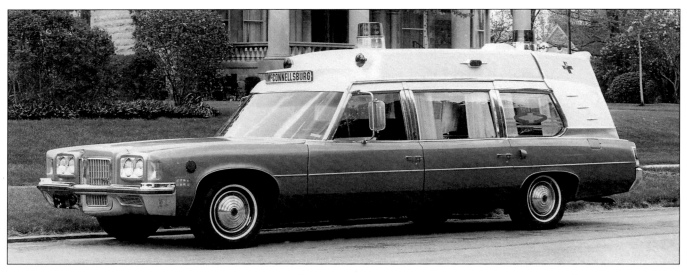

Superior's long-wheelbase Pontiac ambulances now offered the same headroom as the more expensive Cadillacs. This 1972 Superior-Pontiac 54-inch ambulance sports fore-and-aft flattop beacons. Note reflector on left front fender.

Bernie DeWinter IV of Dayton, Ohio is the proud owner of this luxurious 1973 Superior-Cadillac Crown Sovereign limousine combination retired by Van Horn Funeral Home in Lakeview, Ohio in 1991. Note formal swag-type drapes, dual orange roof beacons.

Southern California Chapter member Sonny Schrader's big, white 1973 Miller-Meteor Cadillac Lifeliner at "American Heroes" meet near Los Angeles. Signals include B&M Super Chief siren, four beacons, two electronic siren/speakers, two M/M Full-Vu roof lights.

Big, white 1973 Cotner/Bevington/Oldsmobile Cotington 48-inch hightop ambulance owned by Gene Smith, Granger, Illinois. Note triple roof beacons, white and red tunnel lights.

Below. How's this for a mega-ambulance? Huge custom-built tandem-axle Crown Coach transported patients to and from famed Walter Reed Army Medical Center in Washington, D.C.

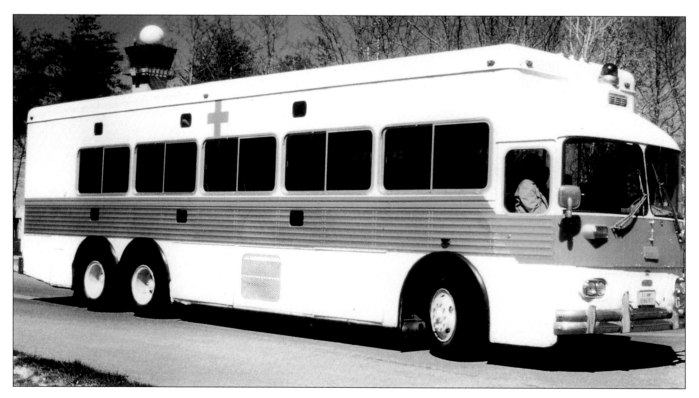

Opposite page bottom. Rear view of 1973 Superior-Pontiac 54-inch headroom ambulance. Canted, side-mounted "scene" or "ditch" lights illuminated accident scene.

1974 Superior-Cadillac Sovereign combination funeral coach/ambulance with distinctive "baronet" rear roof decor. Note big Federal 184 beacon, removable plastic "ambulance" insignia in rear side window.

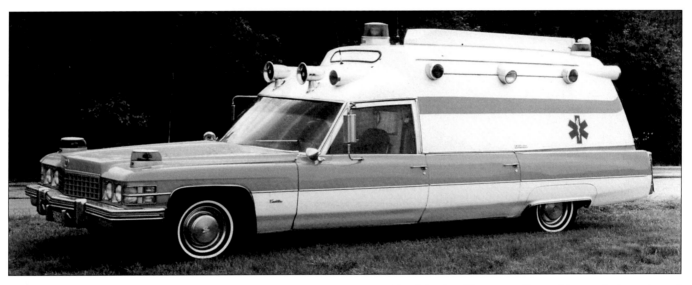

Miller-Meteor's top-line Cadillac rescue-type ambulance was called the M/M Criterion. Floor-to-ceiling cabinets eliminated need for side windows on Tony Karsnia's 1974 Miller-Meteor Cadillac Criterion. Note stretcher/backboard compartment on roof.

Leo Maren owns this awesome silver-over-red 1974 Miller-Meteor Cadillac Criterion, that originally served Long Hill, New Jersey first-aid squad. Note closed rear quarter panel.

Left rear view of Leo Maren's 1974 Miller-Meteor Cadillac Criterion. Note canted "scene" lights, step built into rear bumper, grab handle over rear door.

1974 Cotner/Bevington/Oldsmobile Cotington 48-inch hightop ambulance operated by Kirk's Ambulance Service, Sapulpa, Oklahoma. Note twin clear-lensed beacons, single CP25 electronic siren/speaker.

Below. Another impressive 1974 Miller-Meteor Cadillac Criterion. New "Star of Life" emblem on side indicates compliance with emerging new federal ambulance standards.

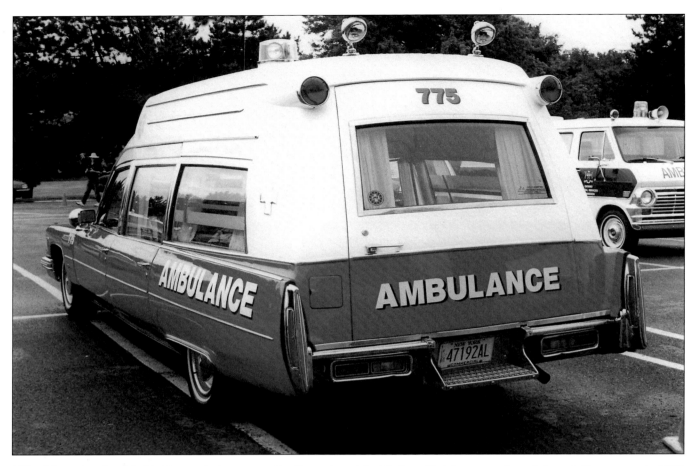

Miller-Meteor's other big hightop ambulance was the limousine-style Lifeliner. Here's a rear view of Joseph Torregrossa's 1974 Miller-Meteor Cadillac Lifeliner.

Peter Graves' white-over-red 1975 Superior-Cadillac 54-inch hightop ambulance originally served Main-Transit Fire Company in western New York. Note Federal Visibar light bar, dual CP25 siren/speakers, illuminated name panel above windshield.

Delivered to American Ambulance in Detroit, this 1975 Superior-Cadillac 54-inch hightop ambulance was never placed into service! The brand new, black-over-white Superior-Cadillac sports chrome grille header.

Superior's answer to Miller-Meteor Criterion and S&S Medic Mark 1 was the big 54XL—as in "extra large." Tom Parkinson photographed the then-new 1975 Superior-Cadillac 54XL operated by Piner Ambulance, Napa, California.

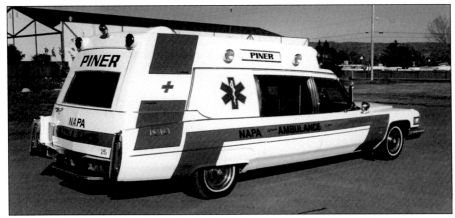

Eye-catching white-over-red 1975 Miller-Meteor Cadillac Criterion ambulance once owned by Terry Lange of Winnipeg, Manitoba, Canada. Note downward-angled "scene" lights on upper body sides.

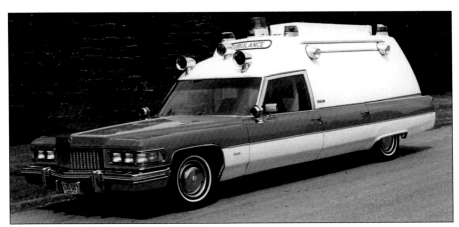

Rear view of 1975 Miller-Meteor Cadillac Criterion which once served Pompton Lakes-Riverdale, New Jersey first-aid squad. These big rescue-type ambulances are popular participants at PCS Meets.

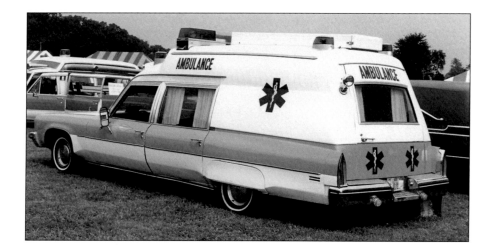

Cotner/Bevington's last year. Featured is a relatively rare 1975 Cotner/Bevington/Oldsmobile Cotington hightop ambulance at a PCS Meet. Note multiple "Star of Life" emblems used in combination with the increasingly popular white and Omaha Orange exterior color.

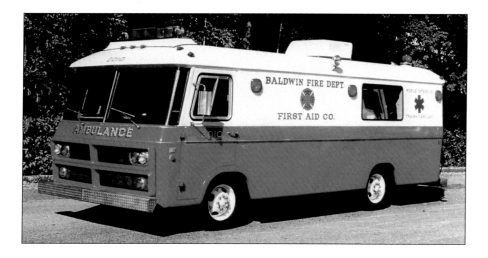

Several companies offered ambulance conversions of Clark Cortez Motor Homes. Steve Lichtman photographed this Grumman/Clark Cortez which served the Baldwin, New York Fire Department.

Below. This would be the last year for really big Cadillac-chassised ambulances. Craig Stewart's 1976 Miller-Meteor Cadillac Lifeliner is a fine example of "the last of the breed."

Rear view of Craig Stewart's impressive 1976 Miller-Meteor Cadillac Lifeliner. Note personalized New Jersey license plate.

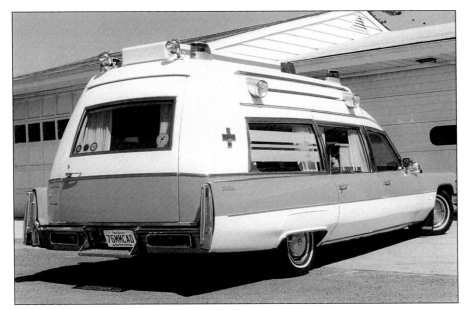

Classic 1976 Miller-Meteor Cadillac Criterion hightop ambulance, Donnell-Wiegand Ambulance Service, Greenville, Illinois. Bill Donnell's big white Criterion sports roof-mounted Federal "Q."

1976 Miller-Meteor Cadillac limousine combination hearse/ambulance owned by Larri Dirks, Sterling, Illinois. No fewer than four big Federal beacon-rays clear the way.

Solid white 1976 Superior-Cadillac 54-inch hightop ambulance owned by Ernie Vattimo, Pittsburgh, Pennsylvania. "The last of the big ones" were powered by Cadillac's 500-cubic-inch V-8 engine.

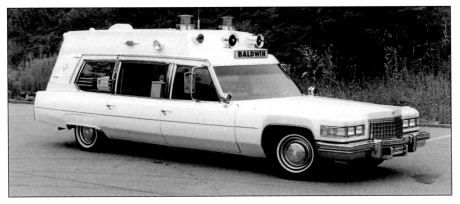

New Jersey first aid and rescue squads preferred big hightop ambulances. Rear view of 1976 Superior-Cadillac "54" which served Elmwood Park, New Jersey.

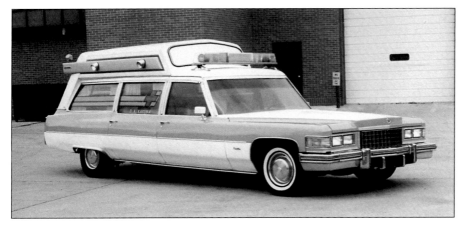

Hess & Eisenhardt built its last S&S ambulances this year. This 1976 S&S Medic Mark 1 was owned by Tony Karsnia, of Roseville, Minnesota.

Below. Some GMC motor home chassis were converted into ambulances and special mobile medical units. Lansing (Michigan) Fire Department EMS used this tandem-axle 1976 GMC motor home conversion powered by a 455-cubic-inch Oldsmobile V-8.

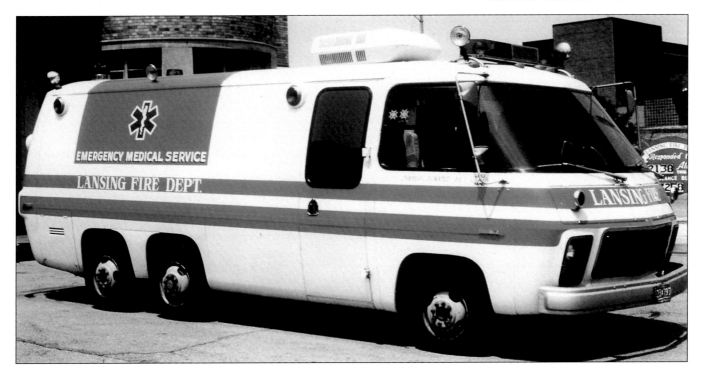

Founded exactly 100 years earlier, S&S ceased ambulance production after its 1976 centennial year. Owned by Scott Smith, Columbia City, Indiana, this 1976 S&S Cadillac Medic Mark 1 was among the last of a long, proud line.

Rear view of Scott Smith's 1976 S&S Medic Mark 1 hightop ambulance. Note rectangular stainless steel tubes incorporating red rear flashers.

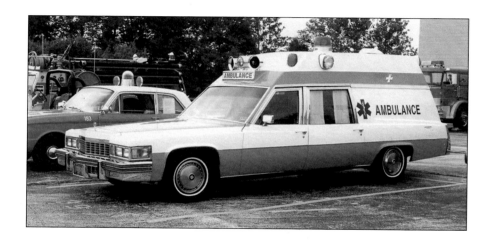

Cadillac ambulance production dwindled with the introduction of the "downsized" 1977 commercial chassis. This 1977 Superior-Cadillac transport ambulance is owned by PCS past-president Mike Barruzza.

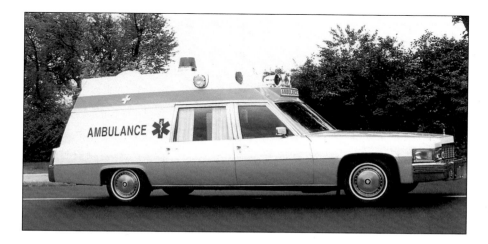

A right-side view of Mike Barruzza's 1977 Superior-Cadillac transport ambulance. Last-generation 1977-1979 Superior-Cadillac ambulances were 51-inch headroom units.

Below. Miller-Meteor's downsized 1977-1978 Cadillac ambulances were all 52-inch headroom Lifeliners. This pristine 1977 Miller-Meteor Cadillac Lifeliner is owned by Warren Waterman of Taylor, Michigan.

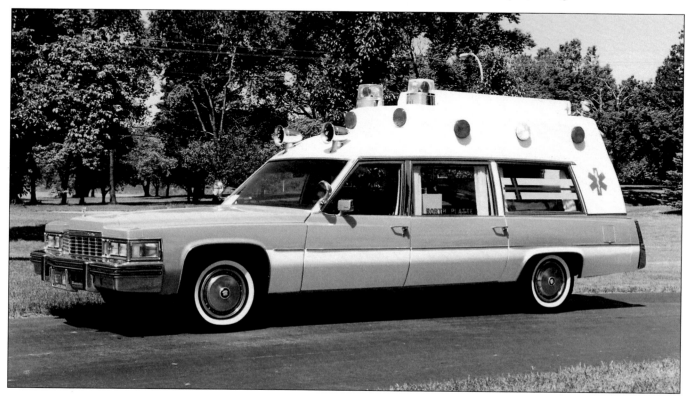

Rear view of downsized 1977 Miller-Meteor Cadillac 52-inch Lifeliner ambulance owned by Scott Crittenden, Windsor Locks, Connecticut. Note fracture board/scoop stretcher compartment on roof.

With downsizing, combination coaches all but disappeared. Funeral Director John Hadley of Marietta, Ohio used this 1977 Miller-Meteor Cadillac classic limousine combination with removable landau hearse panels.

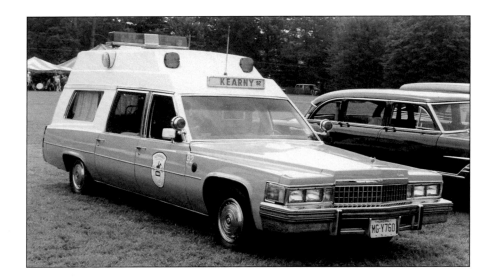

This white-over-blue 1977 Superior-Cadillac transport ambulance photographed at a PCS Meet originally served the Kearney, New Jersey Police Department.

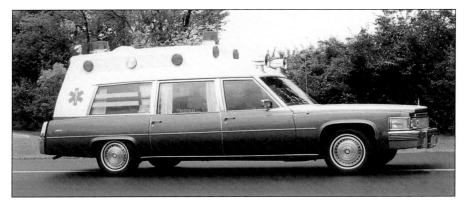

Craig Stewart of Ridgewood, New Jersey owns the last of only four Miller-Meteor Cadillac ambulances built in 1978. Craig's 1978 Miller-Meteor Cadillac Lifeliner was originally used by the Omaha Ambulance Service, Omaha, Nebraska.

Few limousine style professional cars were built after the 1977 downsizing. This 1978 Miller-Meteor Cadillac limousine combination was part of the Maurice Baier Collection, Paxton, Illinois.

This 1978 Superior-Cadillac 51-inch hightop transport ambulance originally owned by Ashland (Ohio) Fire Department now resides on the West Coast.

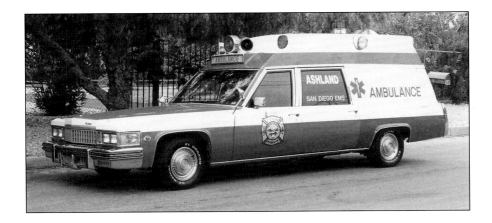

Superior built all of the last passenger car-based ambulances built during the 1979 model year. Clearly marked "transport vehicle," this 1979 Superior-Cadillac transport ambulance served the McAlester, Oklahoma Fire Department.

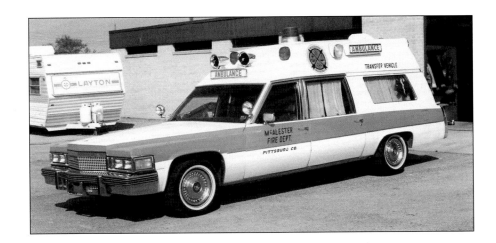

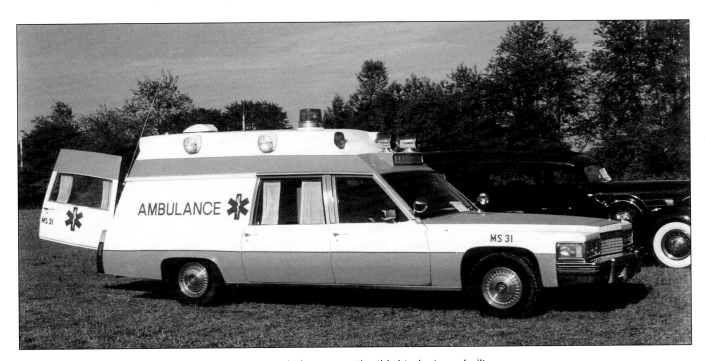

Peter Graves' 1979 Superior-Cadillac transport ambulance was the third-to-last one built.

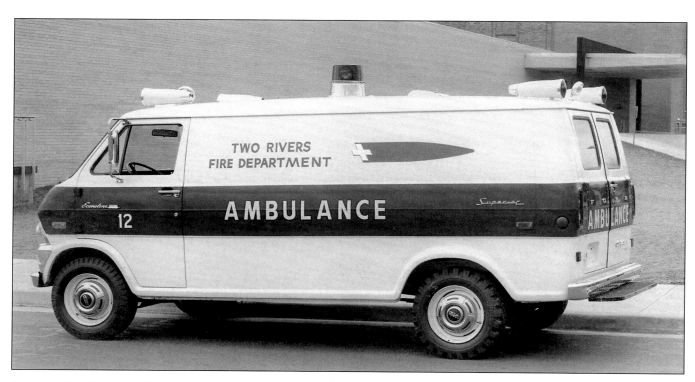

Superior Coach Corporation entered the booming van-type ambulance business with the modified Ford Econoline. This plain 1970 Superior/Ford van ambulance was sold to Two Rivers, Wisconsin.

Typical modern-day "monster" ambulance—2002 Freightliner Fl60 by MedicMaster with extended cab and "big-rig"-style exhaust stacks. Note dressy chrome wheels, bumper-mounted electronic siren.

Vans and Modulars 1970 - 2002

Rarely in automotive industry history has there been such a clear division between the end of **one** era and the affirmation of **another** as there was with the swift demise of the passenger car-based ambulance, and its immediate replacement by two vastly different, far more efficient, **types** of vehicles.

As noted earlier, the first commercially produced motor ambulance in America had made its appearance way back in 1909. The **last** passenger car-based ambulances were built precisely 70 years later—for the 1979 model year.

It is generally believed that the last passenger car-type ambulance built in the United States was a 1979 Superior Cadillac Hightop Transport Ambulance from the Superior Coach Corporation plant in Lima, Ohio, on February 18, 1980 that was delivered to Dr. Roger D. White of Rochester, Minnesota. Dr. White—an outspoken proponent and staunch advocate of the passenger car-type ambulance (and an active member of the Professional Car Society)—personally purchased the milestone 1979 Superior-Cadillac. The van and modular-type ambulances, which had been steadily encroaching on the domain of the traditional passenger car-type over the previous two decades, had triumphed in a big way.

The van and modular ambulance revolution had begun quietly in the early 1960s with the introduction of a new generation of light-duty cargo vans by the Big Three U.S. auto manufacturers. Ford came out with its compact Econoline commercial van in 1961.

Chevrolet immediately countered with its rear-engined, Corvair-based Greenbrier van, which was succeeded a few years later by the more conventional front-engined Chevy Van. Dodge wasn't far behind with its A-Series compact vans and wagons. Although a few firms—notably Automotive Conversion Corporation—soon introduced ambulance conversions of the new small vans, their choppy, truck-like ride and generally anemic engine performance limited their appeal to professional ambulance operators who still preferred the smooth, quiet ride—and the upscale image—of the long-wheelbase passenger car-type unit.

Another vehicle that was making a significant impact on American ambulance design was General Motors' versatile Suburban—essentially a large station wagon built on a light-duty truck chassis. The eight-passenger Suburban had been part of Chevrolet's light truck lineup for many years, and during the 1950s and 1960s more than a few Chevrolet and GMC Suburbans and Carry-Alls were converted into practical, efficient ambulances by a number of conversion companies.

In the late 1950s, International Harvester had entered this growing market with the International Travelall, which also found favor with several ambulance conversion builders. In 1963, the Springfield Equipment Company of Springfield, Ohio, introduced an attractive ambulance conversion of the International Travelall called the **Springfield Interne.**

Built on the standard 119-inch wheelbase, four-door Travelall, the Interne's raised, step-type fiberglass roof offered 51 inches of rear compartment headroom—the same as in the much higher-priced big Cadillacs. A year later Springfield had added a 149-inch wheelbase, 21-inch stretch Interne to its increasingly popular ambulance line.

But it was the arrival of the larger, **next-generation** cargo/passenger vans and the self-contained, modular-type ambulance body, which could be dropped onto a standard light-duty conventional truck chassis, that **really** revolutionized American ambulance design.

The Ford Motor Company announced its all-new, second-generation Econoline Van, Super Van and Club Wagon in 1968. Because of a lengthy strike at Ford that year, deliveries of the new Econoline vans didn't really begin in earnest until the 1969 model year. Available in a deluxe 123-inch wheelbase Super Van variation with V8 power, Ford's

big new Econoline was an instant hit with aftermarket ambulance converters. Ford's E-300 Econoline offered a cavernous interior, excellent ride, handling, and on-road performance making it an attractive and viable alternative to the traditional passenger car-based ambulance.

Chevrolet, which had replaced the 1961-1964 Greenbrier with its more conventional front-engined Chevy Van, responded with a totally new full-sized 1971 Chevy Van and Beaville passenger van with large sliding side door. Not to be outdone, Chrysler Corporation waded into the fray with all-new Dodge Tradesman vans and wagons for 1971. All of these were attractive base vehicles for ambulance conversions.

With the handwriting already on the wall, several of the major U.S. ambulance manufacturers jumped aboard the van-conversion bandwagon. Industry leader Superior

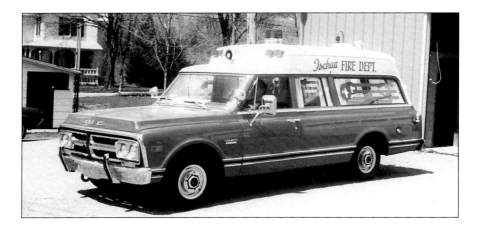

Automotive Conversion Corporation switched from station wagons to Chevrolet and GMC Suburban-type ambulances. This 1972 ACC/GMC ambulance served the Ischua, New York Fire Department.

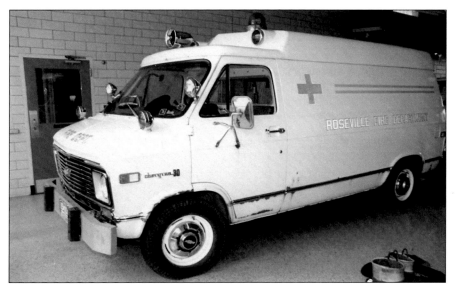

Successor to National Body Manufacturing Company, National Custom Coaches of Knightstown, Indiana also switched from passenger car-type to van and Suburban ambulances. This well-worn 1972 National/Chevy van served the Roseville, Minnesota Fire Department.

Coach was first out of the gate. For 1969, the Lima, Ohio, company complemented its Pontiac and Cadillac ambulance lineup with a modified Ford Econoline van ambulance. This windowless model featured double side and rear doors.

Superior literally "expanded" its van-type ambulance offerings in 1972 with the introduction of its remarkable 61 Series ambulances. The Superior 61 was a Dodge B-300 Maxi or Chevrolet G-30 van that had been sliced down its center line from bumper to bumper and **widened** 14 inches. The result was an exceptionally wide, roomy emergency vehicle. Rival National Custom Coaches also came out with a filleted-and-widened (14 inches) Dodge Maxi Van ambulance conversion called the National Pacemaster 500.

At about the same time, rival Wayne Corporation came out with its very successful **Wayne Sentinel**—a popular raised-headroom

conversion of the Chevrolet Suburban.

The **other** basic vehicle design that was making major inroads in the fast-changing U.S. ambulance industry was the **modular** unit. As its name implied, the **modular ambulance** consisted of a light- or medium-duty conventional truck chassis onto which a separate ambulance "box" or body module was attached. The modular body concept had been widely used by fire departments for light- and medium-duty rescue squad vehicles for some time. These ranged from basic utility-type compartmented bodies bolted to one-ton pickup chassis all the way up to huge, custom-built rescue bodies mounted on heavy-duty truck chassis such as Macks, Internationals, C-Series tilt-cab Fords and Kenworths.

The major advantage of the modular concept was **replaceability**. When the truck chassis was wrecked in an accident, outdated

Superior Coach also offered van-type ambulance conversions of big Chevy vans. Here's one of two 1975 Superior/Chevy vans operated by the Metropolitan Toronto (Canada) Ambulance Service.

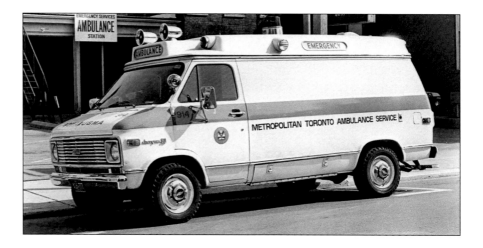

Among the most unique van-type ambulance conversions was Superior's extra-wide "61." Ford, Chevrolet and Dodge vans were split down the center and widened 14 inches. This 1975 Superior/Chevrolet 61 served Livonia, Michigan Fire/Rescue.

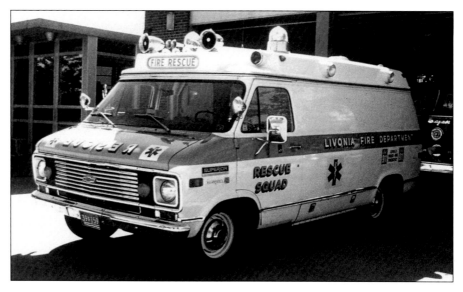

or simply worn out, the body module was unbolted, lifted off and remounted on a new chassis, prolonging indefinitely the service life of the custom-built rescue body.

One of the first major manufacturers of modular-type ambulances was the Horton Company of Columbus, Ohio. Founded in 1968, the Horton Company designed, built and marketed van-type as well as modular ambulances. Another major player in the exploding modular ambulance business was the aptly named Modular Ambulance Corporation of Grand Prairie, Texas.

By the early 1970s, Superior Coach was also offering a modular-type unit. Superior boasted that it already had more than 30 years experience in building modular-type units for the U.S. military.

The revolution in American ambulance design, which is the subject of this chapter, however, was sparked not so much by any general rejection of the passenger car based vehicle as it was by the drafting and implementation—for the first time—of U.S. Federal Government regulations covering basic ambulance design and performance.

In 1966, the National Academy of Sciences had released a study entitled "Accidental Death and Disability In America—The Neglected Disease." This landmark study concluded that emergency medical service in the United States was poor or virtually non-existent, and that in most parts of the country ambulance personnel were providing service with little or no first-aid training or equipment. Few hospitals had the emergency resources to properly deal with seriously injured patients. In perhaps its most shocking conclusion, the report noted that more Americans were dying on U.S. highways than in the Vietnam War due to lack of medical care at home compared to that rendered on far-off battlefields.

The NAS "White Paper" focused attention on the problem and challenged the Government to develop a plan to improve emergency medical services available to accident victims. As a result, a few years later the U.S. Government indeed began to mandate nationally the improvement of emergency medical care, training and equipment—including Ambulances.

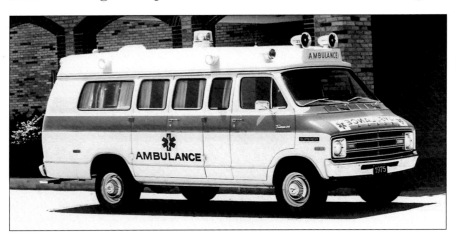

Superior sold extended headroom ambulance conversions of all "Big Three" cargo vans—Ford, Chevrolet and Dodge. Here's a Superior ambulance conversion on a 1975 Dodge Tradesman 200 van chassis.

Among the dozens of companies that entered the exploding van and modular ambulance industry was Midcontinent Conversion Company of Kansas City, Missouri. This is MCC's Stratus II ambulance on a 1977 Dodge B300 Maxivan chassis.

In its study, the National Academy's Committee on Emergency Medical Services of the Division of Medical Sciences had found that most of the ambulances in service in the United States at the time were, "...unsuitable, have incomplete fixed equipment, carry inadequate supplies and are manned by untrained attendants." The committee noted that, "...a true ambulance must provide space for a driver, two attendants and two litter patients so positioned that at least one patient can be given intensive life support during transit: carry equipment and supplies for two-way radio communication for safeguarding personnel and patients under hazardous conditions, for light rescue procedures and for optimal emergency care outside the vehicle and during transport; and be designed and constructed to afford maximum safety and comfort to avoid aggravation of the patient's condition, exposure to complications and threat to survival."

The NAC report was one of several related projects with a common objective—**the development of nationally acceptable standards for ambulance design and the equipment used by ambulance personnel.** The first covered the **training** of ambulance personnel and others responsible for emergency care of the sick and injured at the scene and during transport. The second was concerned with vehicle specifications and the third component of the program translated all of these basic requirements into **engineering and performance specifications** for the production of ambulances that would conform to these requirements.

The report also recommended that ambulances should have, "...a nationally uniform emblem, color, intermittent audible warning signal and a flashing roof light." The move toward a standardized exterior color scheme for ambulances began in earnest in the 1970s. The preferred combination was white with a high-visibility color called **Omaha Orange**, with white as the primary vehicle color accented by bold orange striping and other accents, and the word "Ambulance" prominently displayed on the sides and rear of the vehicle. At about this time, too, someone came up with the idea of placing those nine letters across the front of the vehicle **backwards**—so the word "Ambulance" would be spelled out correctly in the rear-view mirror of the vehicle ahead.

As for a new type of identifying symbol, the Red Cross—long the universal symbol for an ambulance—was replaced by a new ambulance symbol called the **Star of Life.** Beginning in the mid-1970s, the blue three-bar cross with Staff of Aesculapius was used only on ambulances and equipment that met the new Department of Transportation criteria. The Star of Life symbol also certified that the emergency medical care personnel manning the vehicle had been trained to DOT training standards.

What evolved from all this by the early 1970s was U. S. Department of Transportation **Specification KKK-A-1822** which would dramatically change the appearance and configuration of ambulances used in the United States. With the implementation of these new Federal regulations, which mandated basic ambulance design, three distinct **types** of motor ambulances emerged. Three decades later, these same basic vehicle configurations are still in use:

A **Type I Ambulance** is a conventional truck chassis on which a modular-type ambulance body has been mounted.

A **Type II Ambulance** is a van-type ambulance conversion with a raised roof.

A **Type III Ambulance** is a "cutaway" front-section van or RV chassis to which a full-width ambulance body has been added. The Type III ambulance has a walkway between the cab and patient compartment. Some Type I Ambulances also have walk-through capability.

These larger, heavier vehicles offered far more interior space and payload than the outdated passenger car-type units. They were also very cost-competitive, often costing considerably less than a big Cadillac ambulance. Typically, the interior walls of the modern ambulance consist of cabinets and compartments for the vast array of medical equipment and supplies required. Crewmembers could also actually stand up inside the vehicle—something they could **never** do even in the high-headroom car-type units.

Where passenger car-based ambulances underwent annual model changes, making it relatively easy to tell one year and make from

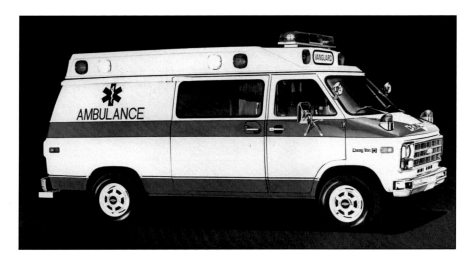

A Wayne Vanguard "Type II" ambulance on a 1978 Chevrolet G-30 van. Note raised roof, big sliding side door, red beacon lights atop front fenders.

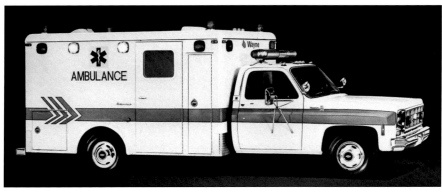

A Wayne Sentinel "Type I" modular ambulance on a 1978 Chevrolet C-30 Silverado chassis. Note Federal Aerodynic light bar, full-length body striping.

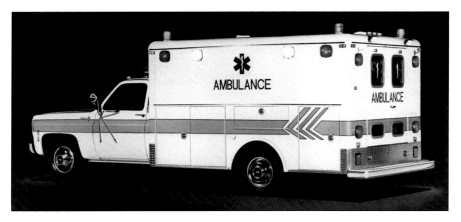

Rear view of a 1978 Wayne Sentinel I modular-type ambulance. Full-width body with big double rear doors made modulars popular with EMT crews.

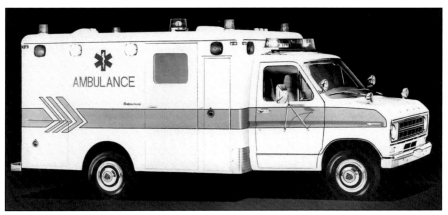

A Wayne Sentinel "Type III" modular ambulance on a 1978 Ford E-350 Chateau cutaway chassis. Note tall equipment compartment to right of rear compartment side door.

another, such was not the case with vans and modulars. With the exception of more aerodynamic chassis and roof styling and integral warning lights, etc., the van or modular-type ambulance of 2002 doesn't look a **whole lot** different than one built in 1980.

Federal Specification KKK-A-1822 also marked a major step in the long-overdue total restructuring of emergency medical service in the United States. The "Triple K" regulations set basic design standards for all new ambulances built and used in the U.S., regardless of whether the emergency medical service (EMS) was provided by local, state or federal governments, volunteers, private contractors or other health care providers.

To meet these new standards, ambulances were required to conform to strict basic design and dimensional criteria as well as the Department of Transportation's Federal Motor Vehicle Safety Standards (FMVSS). Numerous mandatory equipment items had to be carried on all ambulances, and performance capabilities had to be verified by specific tests. A wide range of optional systems, equipment and accessories also had to conform to KKK-A-1822.

Failure to meet these new standards would result in denial of federal funding—increasingly important as more and more funeral directors and private operators discontinued local ambulance service. Most

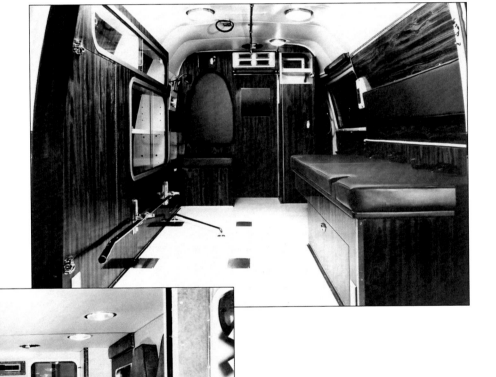

Interior view of a Wayne Vanguard van-type ambulance. Note large equipment cabinets, rear-facing attendant's seat and stretcher lock bar on left, squad bench on right.

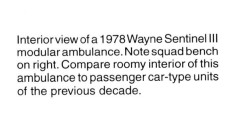

Interior view of a 1978 Wayne Sentinel III modular ambulance. Note squad bench on right. Compare roomy interior of this ambulance to passenger car-type units of the previous decade.

states quickly moved to introduce laws and regulations, which required KKK-A-1822 compliance to qualify for funding.

While this book has focused primarily on the **vehicle**, it is equally important to note the tremendous advances in emergency medical treatment and training which were taking place at this time, and which were largely responsible for the universal shift to van and modular-type ambulances.

For decades, most privately owned and operated ambulances were staffed by dedicated and conscientious—by today's standards—but inadequately trained and equipped attendants. In many instances they were simply employees of the funeral homes who provided ambulance service to the community. In many parts of the country a basic first-aid training course was about all that was required—**if that.** In fairness many volunteer first-aid and rescue squads—particularly in the northeast—took justifiable pride in their quality of service and continuous training, which required their members to take advanced first-aid courses to enhance their knowledge and life-saving skills.

Paralleling the dramatic shift out of passenger car-type ambulances to the heavier, roomier and far more efficient light truck-based units in the late 1960s and early 1970s was the emergence—initially on the West Coast—of the highly-trained **emergency medical technician** (EMT) and the **paramedic,** and the upgrading of local ambulance service to far higher Emergency Medical Service (EMS) standards.

The Los Angeles County Fire Department in the late 1960s largely pioneered the **paramedic/EMT** system in America. Light-duty, truck-based rescue-type ambulances had been widely used in the Los Angeles area long before they were adopted in other areas of the country. If one person can be considered the "father" of today's paramedic system, it is one James O. Page, a former member of the Los Angeles County Fire Department who championed this concept and who later went on to found **JEMS,** a leading journal of emergency medicine.

Ironically, it was a popular **television program** that was in some measure responsible for spreading the paramedic/EMT concept across the nation. First broadcast in 1972, **Emergency!** was a weekly television series which focused on the daily working

A Wayne Medicruiser Type II ambulance on a 1978 Dodge B300 Maxivan chassis.

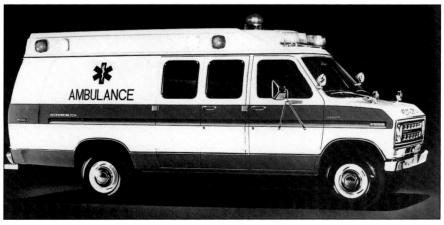

A Wayne Vigilance Type II ambulance on a Ford E-350 super van chassis. Note double side doors and big "West Coast" rear view mirrors on cab doors.

Most Type II van ambulances had raised roofs. This standard headroom 1982 Dodge Ram ambulance was one of a large fleet built for Canadian province of Ontario Ministry of Health by Sentinel, of Cambridge, Ontario (no relation to Wayne).

Oversized tandem-axle Ford Type II ambulance sold by Dietz-McLain specialty vehicles, Anderson, Indiana. Note aerodynamic Plexiglas panel over warning lights above cab.

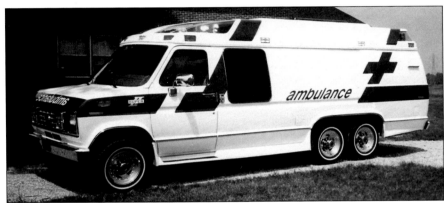

Modular-type ambulances kept getting bigger and bigger. Marion Body Company of Marion, Wisconsin built this tandem-axle Type III ambulance on a 1979 Ford F-series 4x4 chassis for Clarendon Hills, Illinois.

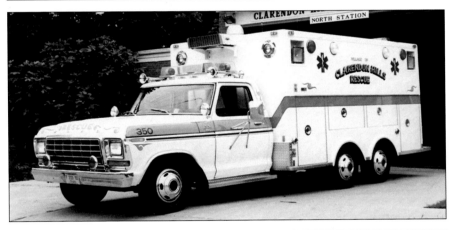

Wheeled Coach Type I ambulance on Chevrolet chassis, Franklin-Bingham Fire Department, Michigan. Note aerodynamic fairing between cab and cube-type modular body.

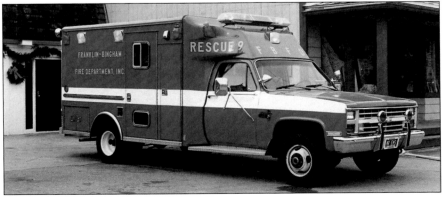

lives of two Los Angeles County Fire Department firefighter/paramedics—John Gage and Roy DeSoto. These two intensely likable characters manned **Squad 51**—a light, utility-bodied rescue unit on a 1972 Dodge D-100 pickup truck chassis, which responded to all kinds of emergencies with L.A. County's fictitious Engine 51. By the time **Emergency!** went off the air some seven years later, the EMT/paramedic concept had been widely adopted across the nation.

Ambulance service in America had undergone a truly massive transformation. The old "scoop-and-run" system had been replaced by far more professional—and successful—treatment administered en route to the hospital or medical center by highly trained emergency medical specialists. The local undertaker owned-and-operated ambulance service had disappeared. More and more fire departments were now providing paramedic EMS service to their communities.

Privately owned and operated ambulance services were becoming a relative rarity. Huge corporate conglomerates—American Medical Response, Medtrans and Laidlaw among them—bought out and consolidated dozens of local and regional ambulance services.

During the 1990s, big V8 gasoline engines were gradually displaced in both van and modular ambulances by a new generation of quiet, efficient diesel powerplants, which offered significant gains in fuel economy. In much the same way the Cadillac commercial chassis once had dominated the professional car industry, Ford now dominates the van-type ambulance business with its ubiquitous E-Series vans and cutaway chassis. On the modular front, Ford, Chevrolet and GMC remain the chassis of choice with North American ambulance builders.

Ambulances are also getting **bigger,** with an increasing number of modular units mounted on medium-duty International and Freightliner chassis/cabs, blurring the line between emergency transport ambulances and heavy rescue squads.

Van or modular, today's extremely well-equipped, high-tech, electronics-laden **Basic Life Support** (BLS), **Advanced Life Support** (ALS), **First Responder** and specialized **Neo-Natal** units are a far cry from the flashy passenger car ambulances of 30 years ago. Utilizing computers, telemetry and ambulance-to-hospital communications undreamed of even a decade ago and manned by highly trained health care professionals who deliver a level of on-scene and in-transit patient care once found only in the emergency wards of major metropolitan hospitals, the modern ambulance is an amazingly efficient mobile lifesaver.

What's the next step in the evolution of the emergency ambulance? Extremely fuel-efficient hybrid powertrains, space-age construction materials to further reduce vehicle weight, and new computer communications in-vehicle equipment and treatment techniques, which would astound the most proficient of today's first-responders, are among the possibilities.

Now entering its fourth century, the humanitarian **Ambulance** remains the noblest of all special-purpose vehicles!

Wheeled Coach became—and still is—one of the major players in the U.S. van and modular ambulance industry. This Wheeled Coach Type II ambulance on a 1985 Ford Econoline chassis served Roger Mills County EMS in Cheyenne, Oklahoma.

Metropolitan Toronto Ambulance Service's custom-built emergency services unit is disaster ambulance conversion of a 1986 Orion Coach. *ESU 5* is equipped to carry 16 stretchers and 10 sitting patients.

1986 Sentinel/Ford Econoline Type II ambulance in service with Sarnia (Ontario) Division of Dow Chemical Corporation.

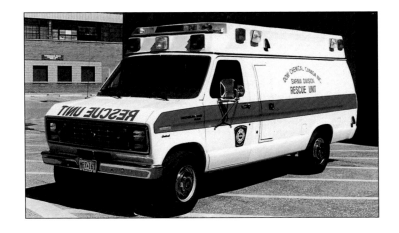

This Type I modular ambulance on a Chevrolet Silverado chassis/cab responds as a fire department ambulance in Lansing, Michigan.

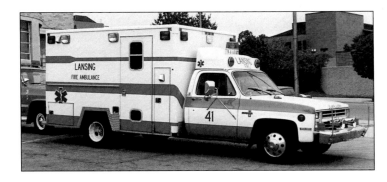

Rear view of high-volume cube-type modular ambulance body on Ford front-section compact cutaway chassis, Dietz-McLain specialty vehicles, Anderson, Indiana.

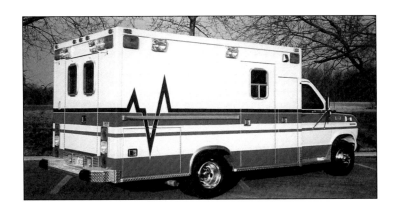

One of eight 1996 Stratus/Chevrolet Type I emergency medical service (EMS) units delivered to the Detroit Fire Department. Note extended front bumper, Code 3 light bar.

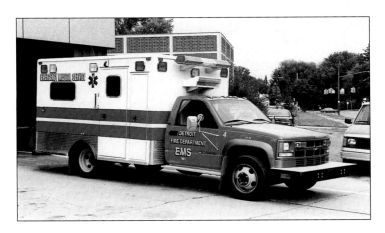

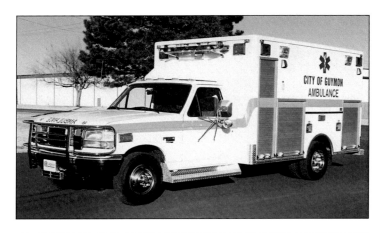

Boardman, an established fire apparatus manufacturer, built ambulances under its own name from 1996 to 1999. This 1996 Type I "walk-through" on a Ford F-350 chassis was built for the Guymon, Oklahoma Police Department.

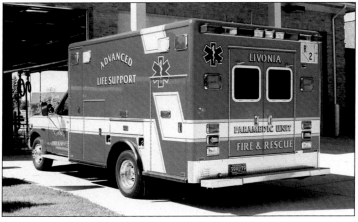

Rear view of Ford-chassised Advanced Life Support (ALS) paramedic unit in service with Livonia, Michigan Fire & Rescue.

1996 Boardman/Ford E-350 Type III ambulance built for Mercy EMS, Nicholls Hills, Oklahoma. Note fire apparatus-type roll-up compartment doors.

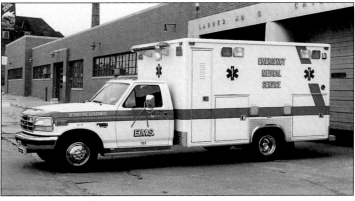

One of ten 1996 Stratus/Ford F-350 "XLT" medic units for the Detroit Fire Department EMS. Code 3 light bar mounted in front of modular body. Color is white with red stripe.

Detroit Fire Department purchased four 1997 Southern Type I modular ambulances on Ford F-350 XLT light-duty truck chassis. These units were fitted with full-width Whelen light bars.

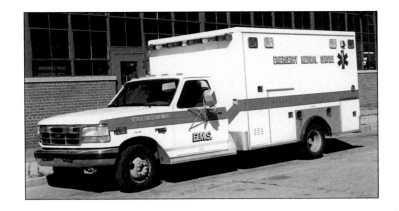

Fire departments provide EMS services in many communities today. Boardman Emergency Vehicles of Clinton, Oklahoma built this Type I ambulance on a 1997 Ford F-350 chassis/cab for Guthrie, Oklahoma Fire/EMS.

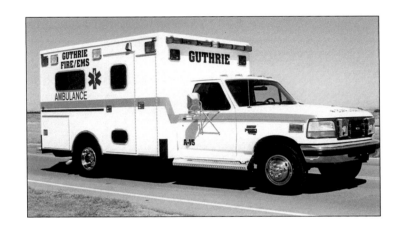

Ford's new aerodynamically styled Econoline chassis made a handsome ambulance. Boardman delivered this 1997 Ford E-350 Type III modular van-type ambulance to Poteau, Oklahoma.

International Harvester competes with Freightliner in the hotly contested medium-duty ambulance chassis market. This International 4000 series Advanced Life Support (ALS) ambulance serves Livonia, Michigan.

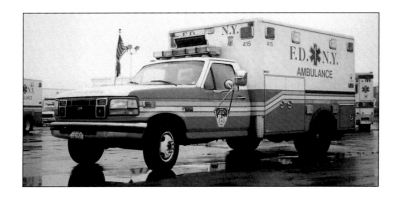

New York City Fire Department (FDNY) purchased 280 Horton/Ford F-series diesel ambulances. This 1997 Horton/Ford is similar to one of five FDNY ambulances destroyed in the World Trade Center attack on September 11, 2001. Five more were heavily damaged.

The New York City Fire Department's huge ambulance fleet also includes 96 of these McCoy-Miller Type III medic units on Ford chassis.

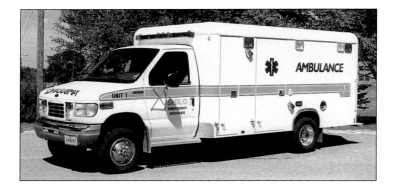

Founded in 1976, Canada's largest ambulance manufacturer is Crestline Coach Ltd. of Saskatoon, Saskatchewan. This 1999 Crestline/Ford Type III ambulance is assigned to the Canadian Forces Base at Shilo, Manitoba, Canada.

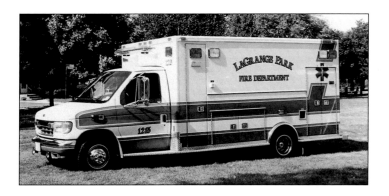

This late-model Type III modular van ambulance on a Ford cutaway chassis serves the LaGrange Park, Illinois Fire Department.

Rear view of one of 17 Wheeled Coach EMS units on a 1999 Ford F-350 XLT chassis, this one assigned to Detroit's busy Medic 6.

"A" is for "ambulance!" Bold blue-on-white graphics adopted by Toronto's Emergency Medical Service. One of 91 Crestline/Ford E-350 diesels delivered to Toronto EMS between 2000 and 2002. Note softly rounded body contours, Whelen light bar.

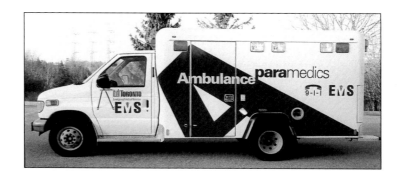

Late-model Type III modular van ambulance—American Emergency Vehicles (AEV) Tomahawk on ubiquitous Ford cutaway chassis. This unit serves Tri-Hospital EMS in Algonac, Michigan.

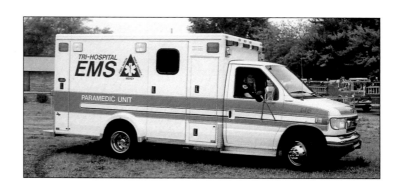

Light- and medium-duty truck chassis continue to get more aerodynamic. Here is one of nine 2001 Wheeled Coach/Ford F-350 XLT Type I units delivered to the Detroit Fire Department.

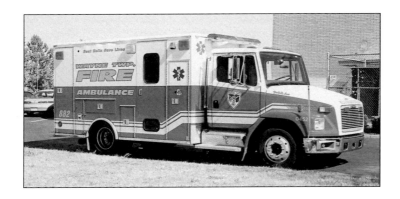

Medium-duty Type I ambulance on Freightliner FL60 chassis operated by Wayne Township, Indiana Fire Department.

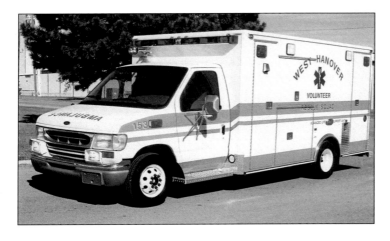

MedicMaster Division of American-LaFrance built this 2001 MedicMaster/Ford E-450 Type III ambulance for West Hanover Volunteer Rescue Squad of Montpelier, Vermont.

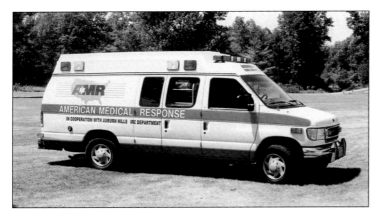

Large conglomerates provide ambulance service in many parts of the United States. American Medical Response (AMR) operates this late-model Ford Type II ambulance in conjunction with Auburn Hills, Michigan Fire Department.

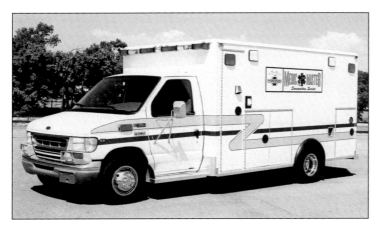

American-LaFrance "Samaritan" ambulance on 2001 Ford E-450 chassis. This unit is an ALF MedicMaster factory demonstrator.

Special disaster services unit used by Canadian Red Cross, London, Ontario, Canada. Del body on 2001 GMC chassis.

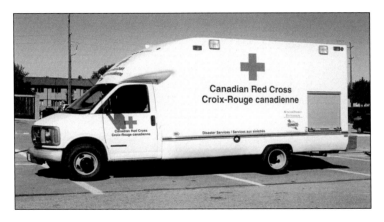

Freightliner/American-LaFrance supplied 22 of these 2002 Sprinter Type II ambulances to the Utah Olympic Public Safety Command during the 2002 Winter Olympics. Sprinter is built in Germany by Mercedes-Benz, a unit of Daimler-Chrysler.

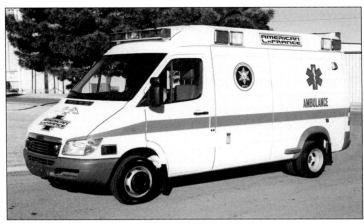

State-of-the-art Type III ambulance—American-LaFrance MedicMaster on a Ford E-450 chassis built for Lima, New York.

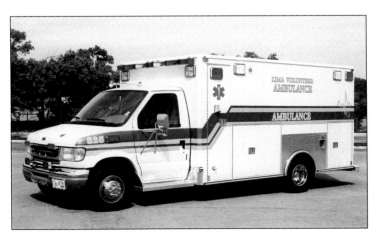

One of five big cube-type modular ambulances built for Anchorage, Alaska. This high-bodied, fire engine red Type I is built on a 2002 Ford E-450 4x4 chassis.

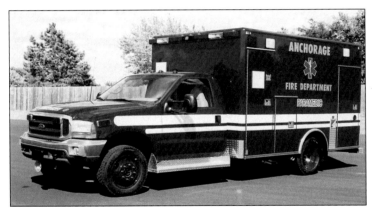

A Roll Call of American Ambulance Manufacturers

PASSENGER CAR-BASED AMBULANCES & COMBINATIONS, PRE-1980:

James Cunningham, Son & Company—Rochester, New York
Crane & Breed Mfg. Company—Cincinnati, Ohio
Sayers & Scovill Company—Cincinnati, Ohio
Hess & Eisenhardt Company—Rossmoyne (Cincinnati), Ohio (Formerly S&S)
Superior Coach Corporation—Lima, Ohio
Studebaker Corporation (Superior Body Company) Lima, Ohio
The Eureka Company—Rock Falls, Illinois
The Henney Motor Company—Freeport, Illinois (formerly John W. Henney Co.)
Acme Coach Company—Sterling, Illinois
The A. J. Miller Company—Bellefontaine, Ohio
The Meteor Motor Car Company—Piqua, Ohio
The Flxible Company—Loudonville, Ohio
Miller-Meteor Division, Wayne Corporation—Piqua, Ohio
Guy Barnette Company—Memphis, Tennessee
The Economy Coach Company—Memphis, Tennessee
The Memphis Coach Company—Memphis, Tennessee (Formerly Economy)
Pinner Coach Company—Olive Branch, Mississippi
Weller Brothers, Inc.—Memphis, Tennessee
National Body Mfg. Company—Knightstown, Indiana
Knightstown Funeral Car Company—Knightstown, Indiana
Silver-Knightstown Funeral Car Company—Knightstown, Indiana
Comet Coach Company—Blytheville, Arkansas
Cotner/Bevington Corporation—Blytheville, Arkansas (Formerly Comet)
Shop of Siebert Associates—Toledo & Waterville, Ohio
National Hearse & Ambulance Company—Toledo, Ohio (Siebert)
Trinity Coach Company—Duncanville, Texas
Automotive Conversion Corporation—Birmingham & Troy, Michigan
Richard Brothers—Eaton Rapids, Michigan (Brierian)
White Motor Company—Cleveland, Ohio
Bender Body Company—Cleveland & Elyria, Ohio
Crown Coach Corporation—Los Angeles, California
E. M. Miller Company—Quincy, Illinois
Keystone Vehicle Company—Columbus, Ohio
Owen Brothers—Lima, Ohio
Holcker Mfg. Company—Kansas City, Missouri
Rock Falls Mfg. Company—Rock Falls, Illinois
Ambulance Imports, Inc.—Warsaw, Indiana (Miesen/Mercedes-Benz 190)

York-Hoover Wagon Company—York, Pennsylvania
Riddle Carriage & Hearse Company—Ravenna, Ohio
Kunkel Carriage Works—Galion, Ohio
Copple Auto Body Works—Los Angeles, California
Leo Gillig Auto Body Works—San Francisco, California
Michigan Hearse & Carriage Company—Grand Rapids, Michigan
Kissel Motor Car Company—Hartford, Wisconsin
National Casket Company (Henney-Kissel) Boston, Massachusetts
Auburn Automobile Company—Auburn, Indiana
Gardener Motor Car Company—St. Louis, Missouri

VAN & MODULAR AMBULANCES—THE INDUSTRY TODAY

Horton Emergency Vehicles—Grove City, Ohio
Wheeled Coach Industries, Inc.—Winter Park, Florida
McCoy-Miller, Inc.—Sturgis, Michigan
American Emergency Vehicles, Inc.—Jefferson, North Carolina (AEV)
Medic Master Vehicle Group—Sanford, Florida
Braun Industries, Inc.—Oakwood, Ohio
Crestline Coach—Saskatoon, Saskatchewan, Canada
Emergency One, Inc.—Ocala, Florida
Emergency Vehicles, Inc.—Lake Park, Florida (EVI)
Excellance, Inc.—Madison, Alabama
Marque, Inc.—Goshen, Indiana
Frazer, Inc.—Houston, Texas
Life Line Emergency Vehicles—Sumner, Iowa
Medevac Ambulance Group—Boucherville, Quebec, Canada
Medtec Ambulance Corp.—Goshen, Indiana (Pierce)
Miller Coach Company, Inc.—Ozark, Missouri
National Ambulance Builders—Orlando, Florida
PL Custom Emergency Vehicles—Manasquan, New Jersey
Road Rescue, Inc.—St. Paul, Minnesota
Swab Wagon Company—Elizabethville, Pennsylvania
Taylor Made Ambulances—Newport, Arkansas
Southern Emergency Vehicles, Inc.—La Grange, Georgia
Osage Ambulances—Linn, Missouri

OTHER PLAYERS:

Hundreds of companies—large and small—have manufactured van and modular-type ambulances over the past 25 years. Many of these firms have since gone out of business or have been acquired or absorbed by competitors or other companies. Some of these firms were very regional in nature, selling their products in a small geographical area. Some professional car distributors and ambulance operators did their own ambulance conversions, or contracted this work out to others. Although it would be nearly impossible to track down *every* concern that built and marketed ambulances following the demise of the passenger car-based unit, the following list provides an overview of this intensely competitive, ever-changing specialty vehicle industry.

Ashley Emergency Vehicles—Jefferson, North Carolina (Now AEV)
Boardman Emergency Vehicles—Clinton, Oklahoma (Division of Sinor Mfg. Co.)
Stratus Specialty Vehicles—Kansas City, Missouri (Mid-continent Conversion Co.)
Modular Ambulance Corporation—Grande Prairie, Texas
First Response, Inc.—Atlanta, Georgia
Frontline Emergency Vehicles—Pinellas Park, Florida
Wayne Corporation—Piqua, Ohio
National Custom Coaches—Knightstown, Indiana

Grumman Health Systems—Melville & Garden City, New York
American Coach Corporation—Watsonville, California
Automotive Conversion Corporation—Troy, Michigan
Parsons Custom Products, Inc.—Parsons, Kansas
Custom Coach International, Inc.—Tulsa, Oklahoma
Springfield Equipment Corporation—Springfield, Ohio
Stoner Industries—Santa Fe Springs, California
Collins Ambulance Corp.—Hutchinson, Kansas
Tec Coach Company—Goshen, Indiana
Cayel-Craft, Inc.—Rock Rapids, Iowa
Mobile Medical—Decatur, Illinois
Roadsafe Emergency Vehicles, Inc.—Shelbyville, Tennessee
Tulsa Custom Coach—Tulsa, Oklahoma
Ampar EMS Division—Fort Wayne, Indiana
First Response, Inc.—Atlanta, Georgia
Challenger Corporation—Memphis, Tennessee
American Coaches, Inc.—Dothan, Alabama
American Emergency Products Co.—Rock Rapids, Iowa
EVF Custom Ambulance & Rescue Vehicles—Riviera Beach, Florida
Star-Line Enterprises, Inc.—Sanford, Florida
Christopher Corporation—New York, New York
Prestige Vehicles, Inc.—Arlington, Texas (Formerly Beck-Rank, Inc.)
REV Roadsafe Emergency Vehicles, Inc.—Shelbyville, Tennessee
Southern Atlantic Ambulance Builders—Daytona Beach, Florida
Mobile Medical Emergency Vehicles, Inc.—Decatur, Indiana
E & E Manufacturers—Colorado Springs, Colorado
Custom Ambulances of Florida Inc.—Lake Park, Florida
Murphy Manufacturing Co.—Wilson, North Carolina
Monticello Safety Equipment—Monticello, Arkansas

CANADIAN AMBULANCE MANUFACTURERS *

B. Greer & Son Company—London, Ontario
Dominion Manufacturers Ltd.—Toronto, Ontario
O. J. Mitchell Company—Ingersoll, Ontario
The Mitchell Hearse Company Ltd.—Ingersoll, Ontario
John J. C. Little Service—Ingersoll, Ontario
Ingersoll Body Corporation—Ingersoll, Ontario
Brantford Coach & Body Co.—Brantford, Ontario (Brantford-Henney)
Smith Motor Bodies Ltd.—Toronto, Ontario
Welles Corporation—Windsor, Ontario
W. S. Ballantine Mfg. Company—Windsor, Ontario
Paul Reaume Conversions—Windsor, Ontario
Sentinel Ambulances—Cambridge, Ontario
Gold Line Conversions—London, Ontario
St. Catharines Auto Bodies Ltd.—St. Catharines, Ontario
Paul Demers Conversions—Beloiel, Quebec *
Tri-Star Industries—Yarmouth, Nova Scotia *
Crestline Coach—Saskatoon, Saskatchewan *
Poudrier & Freres Ltee.—Victoriaville, Quebec

* Still in business today